YPRES, 1914

AN OFFICIAL ACCOUNT PUBLISHED BY
ORDER OF THE GERMAN GENERAL STAFF

TRANSLATION BY G. C. W.

WITH INTRODUCTION AND NOTES BY THE
HISTORICAL SECTION (MILITARY BRANCH)
COMMITTEE OF IMPERIAL DEFENCE

The Naval & Military Press Ltd

Published jointly by
The Naval & Military Press Ltd
Unit 10 Ridgewood Industrial Park,
Uckfield, East Sussex,
TN22 5QE England
Tel: +44 (0) 1825 749494
Fax: +44 (0) 1825 765701
www.naval-military-press.com
www.military-genealogy.com

and

The Imperial War Museum, London
Department of Printed Books
www.iwm.org.uk

CONTENTS

APPENDIX

ILLUSTRATIONS

SKETCH MAPS IN TEXT

INTRODUCTION

THE German book of which a translation is here given was written in the autumn of 1917 by Captain Otto Schwink, a General Staff Officer, by order of the Chief of the General Staff of the Field Army, and is stated to be founded on official documents. It forms one of a series of monographs, partly projected, partly published, on the various phases of the war, but is the only one that is available dealing with operations in which the British Army was engaged. Several concerned with the Eastern theatre of war have already appeared, and one other entitled 'LIÈGE–NAMUR,' relating to the Western.

Field-Marshal Viscount French, in his book '1914,' has said that the period 27th to 31st October during the first battle of YPRES was 'more momentous and fateful than any other which I directed during my period of service as Commander-in-Chief in the field. 31st October and 1st November will remain for ever memorable in the history of our country, for during those two days no more than a thin and straggling line of tired-out British soldiers stood between the Empire and its practical ruin as an independent first-class Power.' The German account accentuates the truth of Lord French's appreciation of the great peril in which the Army and the Nation stood. It tells us of the enemy's plans, and of the large forces that he brought up with great skill and secrecy to carry them out, and, generally, to use Marshal Foch's expression, lets us 'know what was going on in the other fellow's house.' But it does more than that : unconsciously perhaps, it bears convincing testimony to the fighting powers of the British Army, the determination of its leaders, the extraordinary effectiveness of the fire of its artillery and of its cavalry and infantry, and the skill of its engineers ; for it repeatedly credits Field-Marshal Sir John French with 'reinforcements in abundance,' insists that our troops 'fought desperately for every heap of stones and every pile of bricks before abandoning them,' and definitely records that 'the fact that neither the enemy's commanders nor their troops gave way under the strong pressure we put on them . . . gives us the opportunity to acknowledge that there were men of real worth opposed to us who did their duty thoroughly.' We are further told that the effect of our artillery was such that 'it was not possible to push up reserves owing to heavy artillery fire '; that 'all roads leading to the rear were continuously shelled for a long way back '; that the German 'advancing columns were under accurate artillery fire at long range '; that our shells 'blocked streets and bridges and devastated villages so far back that any regular transport of supplies became impossible.' As regards rifle and machine-gun fire, we are credited with 'quantities of machine-guns,' 'large numbers of machine-guns,' etc. ; with the result that 'the roads were swept by machine-guns '; and that 'over every bush, hedge and fragment of wall floated a thin film of smoke betraying a machine-gun rattling out bullets.' At that date we had no machine-gun units, and there were only two machine-guns on the establishment of a battalion, and of these many had been damaged, and had not yet been replaced ; actually machine-guns were few and far between. The only inference to be drawn is that the rapid fire of the British rifleman, were he infantryman, cavalryman or sapper, was mistaken for machine-gun fire both as regards volume and effect. Our simple defences, to complete which both time and labour had been lacking, became in German eyes ' a well-planned maze of trenches,' 'a maze of obstacles and entrenchments ' ; and we had ' turned every house, every wood and every wall into a strong point ' ; ' the villages of WYTSCHAETE and MESSINES . . . had been converted into fortresses ' (*Festungen*) ; as also the edge of a wood near GHELU-VELT and LANGEMARCK. As at the last-named place there was only a small redoubt with a garrison of two platoons, and the ' broad wire entanglements ' described by the German General Staff were in reality but trifling obstacles of the kind that the Germans ' took in their stride,' [1] the lavish praise, were it not for the result of the battle, might be deemed exaggerated. Part of it undoubtedly is. It is fair, however, to deduce that the German nation had to be given some explanation why the ' contemptible little Army ' had not been pushed straightway into the sea.

The monograph is frankly intended to present the views that the German General Staff wish should be held as regards the battles, and prevent, as their Preface says, the currency of ' the legends and rumours which take such an easy hold on the popular imagina-

---

[1] *See p. 115.*

tion and are so difficult, if not impossible, to correct
afterwards.' One cannot naturally expect the whole
truth to be revealed yet ; that it is not will be seen
from the notes. The elder von Moltke said, when
pressed by his nephews to write a true account of
1870-1—to their future financial advantage—'It can't
be done yet. Too many highly placed personages
(*hohe Herrschaften*) would suffer in their reputations.'
It was not until twenty-five years after the Franco-
Prussian War that Fritz Hönig, Kunz and other
German military historians who had been given access
to the records, were allowed to draw back the veil a
little. The publication of the French General Staff
account began even later. What is now given to
us is, however, amply sufficient to follow the main
German plans and movements ; but the difficulties
that prevented the enemy from making successful
use of the enormous number of troops at his disposal
and his superior equipment in heavy artillery, machine-
guns, aeroplanes, hand-grenades and other trench
warfare material, are untold. Until we learn more
we may fairly attribute our victory to the military
qualities of the British, French and Belgian troops,
and the obstinate refusal of all ranks to admit defeat.

The German General Staff specially claim that the
first battle of YPRES was a German victory, 'for it
marked the failure of the enemy's intention to fall on
the rear of our Western Armies, to free the rich districts
of Northern France and the whole of Belgium,' etc.
etc. Granted that we did so fail, the battle can, on that
General Staff's own evidence, be regarded as a drawn
one. For it is definitely stated in the monograph
that the object of the operations was 'successfully

closing with the enemy . . . and gaining CALAIS, the aim and object of the 1914 campaign '—this the German Army notoriously did not do. The intention to break through is repeatedly stated : 'although fresh reinforcements had been sent up by the German General Staff . . . a break-through had not been possible.' 'Another effort to break through should be made as soon as possible.' We are told that Fabeck's Army Group (eventually nine infantry and five cavalry divisions) was formed ' as a strong new army of attack . . . for breaking through on the front WERWICQ–WARNETON.' Linsingen's Army Group (five divisions) after the failure of von Fabeck was formed ' to drive back and crush the enemy lying north of the (COMINES–YPRES) canal . . . and to break through there.' Finally, however, it is admitted that 'no break-through of the enemy's lines had been accomplished. . . . We had not succeeded in making the decisive break-through, and the dream of ending the campaign in the west in our favour had to be consigned to its grave.' In fact, the book is largely an apologia and a confession of failure which mere protestations of victory cannot alter.

The effects of a German victory on the course of the war, with the Channel ports in German hands, as compared with those of an Allied victory in Flanders, which at that period of the war and at that season of the year could have resulted in little more than pushing the enemy back into Belgium a few miles, may be easily imagined. If the battle was a tactical draw, at least we had a strategic balance in our favour.

The principal reasons advanced for the German ill-success are ' the enemy's numerical superiority, and the strength of his positions,' and of course the drastic course taken by the Belgians of 'calling in the sea to their aid.'

There is constant repetition of these pleas throughout the book. To those who were there and saw our ' thin and straggling line ? and the hastily constructed and lightly wired defences : mere isolated posts and broken lengths of shallow holes with occasional thin belts of wire, and none of the communication trenches of a later date, they provoke only amazement. Even German myopia cannot be the cause of such statements.

As regards the superiority of numbers, the following appears to be the approximate state of the case as regards the infantry on the battle front from ARMEN-TIÈRES (inclusive) to the sea dealt with in the monograph. It is necessary to count in battalions, as the Germans had two or three with each cavalry division, and the British Commander-in-Chief enumerates the reinforcements sent up to YPRES from the II and Indian Corps by battalions, and two Territorial battalions, London Scottish and Hertfordshires, also took part. The total figures are :—

British, French, Belgian   .   .   263 battalions.
German   .   .   .   .   .   426 battalions.

That is roughly a proportion of Allies to Germans of 13 to 21. Viscount French in his ' 1914 ' says 7 to 12 Corps, which is much the same : 52 to 84 as against 49 to 84, and very different from the German claim of ' 40 divisions to 25.' Actually in infantry divisions the Allies had only 22, even counting as complete the Belgian six, which had only the strength of German brigades. Any future correction of the figures, when actual bayonets present can be counted, will probably emphasise the German superiority in numbers still more, and the enemy indisputably had the advantage of united command, homogeneous formations and uniform material which were lacking in the Allied force.

As regards the cavalry the Western Allies had six divisions, including one of three brigades. The enemy had at least nine, possibly more (one, the Guard Cavalry Division, of three brigades), as it is not clear from the German account how much cavalry was transferred from the Sixth Army to the Fourth Army.[1] It may be noted that a German cavalry division included, with its two or three cavalry brigades, horse artillery batteries and the two or three *Jäger* battalions, three or more machine-gun batteries and two or more companies of cyclists ; and was thus, unlike ours, a force of all arms.

The German General Staff reveal nothing about the exact strength of the artillery. In a footnote it is mentioned that in addition to infantry divisions

---

[1] *Fourth Army Cavalry.*

I. Cavalry Corps	.	*Guard* and *4th Cavalry Divisions, p.* 64.
II. ,,	. .	*3rd* and *7th Cavalry Divisions, p.* 90.
IV. ,,	. .	*3 Cavalry Divisions, p.* 25.
		2nd Cavalry Division, p. 92.
		Bavarian Cavalry Division, p. 92.

Total, 9 *Cavalry Divisions.*

The Army Cavalry of the Sixth Army is stated on p. 56 *to have been eight divisions, among which, according to p.* 57, *were the 3rd, 7th and Bavarian Cavalry Divisions, included above in the Army Cavalry of the Fourth Army.*

It may be noted that in ' Liège–Namur' in the same series of General Staff Monographs the composition of the II Cavalry Corps is given as the 2nd, 4th and 9th Cavalry Divisions.

the III Reserve Corps contained siege artillery, *Pionier* formations and other technical troops ; and in the text that ' all the available heavy artillery of the Sixth Army was to be brought up (to assist the Fourth Army) for the break-through.' The Germans had trench-mortars (*Minenwerfer*) which are several times mentioned, whilst our first ones were still in the process of improvisation by the Engineers of the Indian Corps at BETHUNE.

The statement that ' the enemy's ' (*i.e.* British, French and Belgian) ' superiority in material, in guns, trench-mortars, machine-guns and aeroplanes, etc., was two, three, even fourfold ' is palpably nonsense when said of 1914, though true perhaps in 1917 when the monograph was written.

The fact seems to be that the Germans cannot understand defeat in war except on the premise that the victor had superiority of numbers. To show to what extent this creed obtains : in the late Dr. Wylie's *Henry V.*, vol. II. page 216, will be found an account of a German theory, accepted by the well-known historian Delbrück, that the English won at Agincourt on account of superior numbers, although contemporary history is practically unanimous that the French were ten to one. Dr. Wylie sums it up thus :

' Starting with the belief that the defeat of the French is inexplicable on the assumption that they greatly outnumbered the English, and finding that all contemporary authorities, both French and English, are agreed that they did, the writer builds up a theory that all the known facts can be explained on the supposition that the French were really much inferior to us in numbers . . . and concludes that he cannot be far wrong if he puts the total number of French (the English being 6000) at something between 4000 and 7000.'

It may not be out of place to add that a German Staff Officer captured during the Ypres fighting said to his escort as he was being taken away : ' Now I am out of it, do tell me where your reserves are concealed ; in what woods are they ? ' and he refused to believe that we had none. Apparently it was inconceivable to the German General Staff that we should stand to fight unless we had superior numbers ; and these not being visible in the field, they must be hidden away somewhere.

Further light on what the Germans imagined is thrown by prisoners, who definitely stated that their main attack was made south of YPRES, because it was thought that our main reserves were near ST. JEAN, north-east of that town. From others it was gathered that what could be seen of our army in that quarter was in such small and scattered parties that it was taken to be an outpost line covering important concentrations, and the Germans did not press on, fearing a trap.

It is, however, possible that the German miscalculation of the number of formations engaged may not be altogether due to imaginary reserves, as regards the British Army. Before the war the Great General Staff knew very little about us. The collection of ' intelligence ' with regard to the British Empire was dealt with by a Section known in the Moltkestrasse as the ' Demi-monde Section,' because it was responsible for so many countries ; and this Section admittedly had little time to devote to us. Our organisation was different from that of any of the great European armies. Their field artillery brigades contained seventy-two guns, whereas ours had only eighteen guns or howitzers ; their infantry brigades consisted of two regiments, each of three battalions, that is six battalions, not four as in the original British Expeditionary Force. To a German, therefore, an infantry brigade meant six battalions, not four, and if a prisoner said that he belonged to the Blankshire Regiment, the German might possibly believe he had identified three battalions, whereas only one would be present.   This is actually brought out on page 118, when the author speaks of the 1st Battalion of the King's (Liverpool) Regiment as the *Königsregiment Liverpool,* and indicates his ignorance of the British Army, when this single battalion engages the German *Garde Regiment zu Fuss,* by describing the fight not only as one of regiment against regiment, but as *Garde gegen Garde* (Guard against Guards).[1]   Such is the fighting value of an English Line battalion.   A victory over it is certainly claimed, but the significant sentence immediately follows : ' any further advance on the 11th November by our Guard troops north of the road was now out of the question.'

It may be as well to point out that the ' volunteers ' who it is said flocked to the barracks to form the Reserve Corps XXII to XXVII were not all volunteers in our sense of the word.   The General Staff only

---

[1] *There is a further mistake (see footnote 2, p. 118) : the King's were not present at the place referred to, but in another part of the field.   The honour of fighting the German Guards at one to eight, for the battalion was under four hundred strong, appears to belong to the 2nd Oxfordshire and Buckinghamshire Light Infantry.*

claims that 75 per cent. were untrained, a very different state of affairs from our New Armies, which had not 1 per cent. of trained soldiers. Many of the 'volunteers' were fully trained men liable to service, who merely anticipated their recall to the colours. It was well known before the war that in each army corps area Germany intended to form one 'Active' Corps and one or more 'Reserve' Corps. The original armies of invasion all contained Reserve Corps notably the IV Reserve of von Kluck's Army, which marched and fought just as the active ones did. These first formed Reserve Corps were, it is believed, entirely made up of trained men, but those with the higher numbers XXII, XXIII, XXVI and XXVII, which appear in the Fourth Army, probably did contain a good percentage of men untrained before the war.

Ersatz divisions were formed of the balance of reservists after the Reserve divisions had been organised, and of untrained men liable for service. After a time the words 'Active,' 'Reserve,' and '*Ersatz*' applied to formations lost their significance, as the same classes of men were to be found in all of them.

No attempt has been made to tone down the author's patriotic sentiments and occasional lapses from good taste ; the general nature of the narrative is too satisfactory to the British Army to make any omissions necessary when presenting it to the British public.

The footnotes deal with a number of the more important points raised, but are not exhaustive.

Note.—The German time, at the period of the year in question one hour earlier than ours, has been adhered to.

The Notes of the Historical Section are distinguished from those of the Author by being printed in italics.

In preparing the translation for issue it has not been thought necessary to supply all the maps provided in the original, as the general lie of the country must be fairly well known to British readers.

(*Translation of Title Page*)

Monographs on the Great War

———

THE BATTLE ON THE YSER AND OF
YPRES IN THE AUTUMN 1914

(DIE SCHLACHT AN DER YSER UND
BEI YPERN IM HERBST 1914)

FROM OFFICIAL SOURCES

PUBLISHED
BY ORDER OF THE GERMAN GENERAL STAFF
OLDENBURG, 1918, GERHARD STALLING

PREFACE

By German Great Headquarters

THE gigantic scale of the present war defies comparison with those of the past, and battles which formerly held the world in suspense are now almost forgotten. The German people have been kept informed of the progress of events on all fronts since the 4th August 1914, by the daily official reports of the German General Staff, but the general public will have been unable to gather from these a coherent and continuous story of the operations.

For this reason the General Staff of the German Field Army has decided to permit the publication of a series of monographs which will give the German people a general knowledge of the course of the most important operations in this colossal struggle of nations.

These monographs cannot be called histories of the war; years, even decades, must pass before all the true inwardness and connection of events will be completely revealed. This can only be done when the archives of our opponents have been opened to the world as well as our own and those of the General Staffs of our Allies. In the meantime the German people will be given descriptions of the most important of the battles, written by men who took part in them, and have had the official records at their disposal.

It is possible that later research may make alterations here and there necessary, but this appears no reason for delaying publications based on official documents, indeed to do so would only serve to foster the legends and rumours which so easily take hold of the popular imagination and are so difficult, if not impossible, to correct afterwards.

This series of monographs is not therefore intended as an addition to military science, but has been written for all classes of the German public who have borne the burden of the war, and especially for those who have fought in the operations, in order to increase their knowledge of the great events for the success of which they have so gladly offered their lives.

GENERAL STAFF OF THE FIELD ARMY.

GERMAN GREAT HEADQUARTERS,
Autumn, 1917.

YPRES, 1914

PRELIMINARY REMARKS

THERE is no more brilliant campaign in history than the advance of our armies against the Western Powers in August and early September 1914. The weak French attacks into Alsace, the short-lived effort to beat back the centre and right wing of our striking-force, the active defence of the Allied hostile armies and the passive resistance of the great Belgian and French fortresses, all failed to stop our triumphal march. The patriotic devotion and unexampled courage of each individual German soldier, combined with the able leading of his commanders, overcame all opposition and sent home the news of countless German victories. It was not long before the walls and hearts of Paris were trembling, and it seemed as if the conspiracy which half the world had been weaving against us for so many years was to be brought to a rapid conclusion. Then came the battle of the Marne, in the course of which the centre and right wings of the German Western Army were, it is true, withdrawn, but only to fight again as soon as possible, under more favourable strategic conditions. The enemy, not expecting our withdrawal, only followed slowly, and on 13th September [1] our troops brought him to a standstill along a line extending from the Swiss frontier to the Aisne, north-east of Compiègne. In the trench warfare

---

[1] *The British advance was checked on the Aisne on 14th, not 13th September,*

A

which now began our pursuers soon discovered that our strength had been by no means broken, or even materially weakened, by the hard fighting.

As early as 5th September, before the battle of the Marne, the Chief of the German General Staff had ordered the right wing should be reinforced by the newly-formed Seventh Army.* It soon became clear to the opposing commanders that any attempt to break through the new German front was doomed to failure, and that a decisive success could only be obtained by making an outflanking movement on a large scale against the German right wing. Thus began what our opponents have called the 'Race to the Sea,' in which each party tried to gain a decision by outflanking the other's western wing. The good communications of France, especially in the north, enabled the Allied troops to be moved far more rapidly than our own, for the German General Staff had at their disposal only the few Franco-Belgian railways which had been repaired, and these were already over-burdened with transport of material of every description. In spite of this, however, the French and British attacks failed to drive back the German right wing at any point. Not only did they find German troops ready to meet them in every case, but we were also generally able to keep the initiative in our hands.

In this manner by the end of September the opposing flanks had been extended to the district north of the Somme, about Péronne–Albert. A few days later began the interminable fighting round Arras and Lens,

---

* The Seventh Army was not put in on the extreme right wing but between the First and Third Armies after the heavy French attacks south of Laon in the middle of September.

and by the middle of October our advanced troops were near Lille, marching through the richest industrial country of France. The Army Cavalry was placed so as to threaten the hostile left flank, and to bring pressure against the communications with England. Our cavalry patrols pushed forward as far as Cassel and Hazebrouck, the pivots of the enemy's movements, but they had to retire eastwards again when superior hostile forces moved up to the north-east. The reports which they brought back with them all pointed to preparations by the enemy for an attack on a large scale, and for another effort to turn the fortunes of the campaign to his favour. With this in view all available troops, including newly-arrived detachments from England, were to be used to break through the gap between Lille and Antwerp against our right wing, roll it up and begin the advance against the northern Rhine.

It must be remembered that at the time this plan was conceived the fortresses of Lille and Antwerp were still in French and Belgian possession. It was hoped that Lille, with its well-built fortifications, even though they were not quite up-to-date, would at least hold up the German right wing for a time. Antwerp was defended by the whole Belgian Army of from five to six divisions which were to be reinforced by British troops, and it was confidently expected that this garrison would be sufficiently strong to hold the most modern fortress in Western Europe against any attack, especially if, as was generally believed, this could only be carried out by comparatively weak forces. Thus it seemed that the area of concentration for the Franco-Belgian masses was secure until all preparations were ready for the blow to be delivered through weakly-held Belgium against the rear of the German armies in the west. The plan was a bold one, but it was countered by a big attack of considerable German forces in the same neighbourhood and at the same time. The two opponents met and held each other up on the Yser and at Ypres, and here the last hope of our enemy to seize Belgium and gain possession of the rich provinces of Northern France before the end of the year was frustrated. The question arises how the Germans were able to find the men to do this, since it had been necessary to send considerable forces to the Eastern front to stop the Russian advance.

Whoever has lived through those great days of August 1914, and witnessed the wonderful enthusiasm of the German nation, will never forget that within a few days more than a million volunteers entered German barracks to prepare to fight the enemies who were hemming in Germany. Workmen, students, peasants, townspeople, teachers, traders, officials, high and low, all hastened to join the colours. There was such a constant stream of men that finally they had to be sent away, and put off till a later date, for there was neither equipment nor clothing left for them. By 16th August, before the advance in the west had begun, the Prussian War Minister in Berlin had ordered the formation of five new Reserve Corps to be numbered from XXII to XXVI, whilst Bavaria formed the 6th Bavarian Reserve Division, and Saxony and Würtemburg together brought the XXVII Reserve Corps into being. Old and young had taken up arms in August 1914, in their enthusiasm to defend their

country, and 75 per cent. of the new Corps consisted
of these volunteers, the remainder being trained men
of both categories of the *Landwehr* and the *Landsturm,*
as well as some reservists from the depôts, who joined
up in September. All these men, ranging from sixteen
to fifty years of age, realised the seriousness of the
moment, and the need of their country : they were
anxious to become useful soldiers as quickly as possible
to help in overthrowing our malicious enemies. Some
regiments consisted entirely of students ; whole classes
of the higher educational schools came with their
teachers and joined the same company or battery.
Countless retired officers placed themselves at the
disposal of the Government, and the country will
never forget these patriots who took over commands
in the new units, the formation of which was mainly
due to their willing and unselfish work.

The transport of the XXII, XXIII, XXIV, XXVI
and XXVII Reserve Corps to the Western Front began
on 10th October, and the 6th Bavarian Reserve Division followed shortly after. Only comparatively few
experienced commanders were available for the units,
and it was left to their keen and patriotic spirit to
compensate as far as possible for what the men still
lacked to play their part in the great struggle.

The situation of the armies on the Western Front
at this time was as follows. In the neighbourhood of
Lille the northern wing of the Sixth Army was fighting against an ever-increasing enemy. On 9th October,
Antwerp, in spite of its strong fortifications and
garrison, was taken after a twelve days' siege directed
by General von Beseler, commanding the III Reserve
Corps, and well known in peace time as Chief of the

Engineer Corps and Inspector-General of Fortifications. The victorious besiegers had carried all before them. As they were numerically insufficient to invest Antwerp on the west, south and east, a break-through was attempted on a comparatively narrow front. It was completely successful, and Antwerp was occupied ; but the main body of the Belgian army, in good fighting order, was able to escape westwards along the coast, to await the arrival of British and French reinforcements behind the Yser. Only about 5000 Belgians were taken prisoner, but some 20,000 Belgian and 2000 British troops [1] were forced into Holland. In consequence of this new situation, and of the reports of hostile concentrations in the area Calais–Dunkirk–Lille, the German General Staff decided to form a new Fourth Army under Duke Albert of Würtemburg. It was to be composed of the XXII, XXIII, XXVI, and XXVII Reserve Corps,* and was joined later on by the III Reserve Corps with the 4th *Ersatz* Division. By 13th October the detrainment of this new Army was in full progress west and south-west of Brussels. On the evening of 14th October the four Reserve Corps began their march to the line Eecloo (fifteen miles east of Bruges)–Deynze—point four miles west of Audenarde.

In the meantime we had occupied the fortified town of Lille. It had been entered on 12th October by part of the XIX Saxon Corps and some *Landwehr* troops, after the town had suffered considerably owing to the useless efforts of French territorial troops to

---

* The XXIV Reserve Corps was sent to the neighbourhood of Metz.

[1] ' 2000 *British* ' *belonged to the newly raised Royal Naval Division which had been thrown into Antwerp in the endeavour to prolong the resistance of that fortress.*

defend it. The order to the garrison was: ' The town
is to be held till the Tenth French Army arrives '; it
resulted in the capture of 4500 French prisoners, who
were sent to Germany. On the 14th the right wing
of the Sixth Army, consisting of the XIII Würtemburg and XIX Saxon Corps, pushed forward to the
Lys, behind a screen of three Cavalry Corps.[1] They
took up a position covering Lille, from Menin through
Comines to Warneton and thence east of Armentières,
where they came into touch with the 14th Infantry
Division which was further south near the western
forts of Lille. To the north of the Sixth Army, the
III Reserve Corps, with its three divisions from
Antwerp, was advancing westwards on a broad front.
By the 14th it had driven back the hostile rearguards
and reached a line from Bruges to near Ghent. Airmen
and reconnaissance detachments had recognised movements of large bodies of troops about Hazebrouck,
Lillers and St. Omer and reported disembarkations
on a big scale at Dunkirk and Calais. In addition to
this, considerable hostile forces had reached Ypres,
and appeared to be facing more or less southwards
opposite the northern wing of the Sixth Army.[2]

An order issued on 14th October, by the Chief of the
German General Staff, gave the following instructions
for the German forces between Lille and the sea. The
Sixth Army was at first to remain entirely on the
defensive along the line Menin–Armentières–La Bassée

---

[1] *Only the British III Corps and Cavalry Corps of two Divisions
were available to oppose them.*

[2] *These ' considerable hostile forces ' consisted of the 7th Division and
Byng's Cavalry Division, which reached Ypres on 14th October, after
having moved up to Ghent to help cover the retreat of the Belgian army
from Antwerp.*

and to await the attack of our new Fourth Army against the left flank of the enemy. The offensive action of the Fourth Army after its deployment was to be so directed that the III Reserve Corps, which now belonged to it, should move as its right wing in echelon along the coast, whilst its left was to advance through Menin.

In accordance with these orders the III Reserve Corps occupied Ostend on the 15th, its left wing reaching the line of the Thourout–Roulers road. The Corps was then ordered not to advance further for a few days, so as to avoid the attention of the British and French, who were advancing against the north wing of the Sixth Army, being drawn prematurely to movements in this neighbourhood. Only patrols therefore were sent out to reconnoitre across the Yser and the canal south of it. On the 17th the XXII, XXIII, XXVI and XXVII Reserve Corps reached the line Oostcamp (south of Bruges)–Thielt—point six miles east of Courtrai. On the advance of these four new Corps, the III Reserve Corps was to draw away to the right wing, and during the 17th and the following morning it moved up to the sector of attack allotted to it immediately south of the coast, and cleared the front of the Fourth Army. The reconnaissance activity of the previous days had in places led to severe fighting, especially on the southern wing in front of the 6th Reserve Division. It was found that the Belgian rearguards still held part of the ground east of the Yser and of the canal to Ypres. Any attempt to advance beyond this water-barrier was out of the question, as the bridges had been blown up and the whole line put in a state of defence.

The screening of the advancing Fourth Army by the III Reserve Corps was a brilliant success. At midday on the 18th, Field-Marshal French, who was to direct the enemy's attack from the line of the Yser, was still in ignorance of our new Army. He believed he had time to prepare for his attack, and his only immediate care was to secure the line from Armentières to the sea for the deployment. After the events on the Marne, Field-Marshal French had particularly requested General Joffre, the Allied commander,[1] that he might be placed on the northern flank of the line. He would then be close to Calais, which had already become an English town,[2] he would be able to protect the communications to his country ; and, further, the fame to be gained by a decisive and final victory attracted this ambitious commander to the north. As a result the II British Corps under General Smith-Dorrien was now in action against the strong German positions between Vermelles (four miles south-west of La Bassée) and Laventie (west of Lille).[3] Further to the north the III British Corps was fighting against the Saxons advancing from Lille and our I, II and IV Cavalry Corps.[4] The I British Cavalry Corps was covering the

---

[1] *Needless to point out that General Joffre was never ' Allied Commander.'*

[2] *At this date Calais had not yet become a base for the British army, and there were no British establishments of any kind there.*

[3] *The II Corps completed its detrainment at Abbeville on 8th October, and moved forward, covered by the cavalry, on the 11th ; by the 18th it had reached the line Givenchy–Villaines–Lorgies–Herlies after considerable fighting.*

[4] *On 18th October the III Corps had its left Division, the 4th, astride the Lys from Ploegsteert Wood to Frelinghien, while the 6th Division on the right had reached the line Premesques–Ennetières–Radinghem (S.E. of Armentières). General Conneau's French Cavalry Corps filled the gap between its right and the left of the II Corps.*

hostile advance on the line Messines–Gheluvelt, south-east of Ypres.[1] Immediately to the north again, the newly formed IV British Corps, consisting of the 7th Infantry Division and 3rd Cavalry Division, had arrived in the area Gheluvelt–Zonnebeke, pursued in its retreat by von Beseler's columns (III Reserve Corps). On its left the I British Corps had marched up to Bixschoote,[2] and the gap between this place and Dixmude had been closed by a French Cavalry Division which connected up with the Belgian Army. The last, reinforced by two French Territorial divisions, was engaged in preparing the line of the Yser up to the sea for the most stubborn defence. These strong forces were to cover the arrival of the VIII and X French Corps [3] and were to deliver the first blow against our supposed right wing.

On the 18th one of our cyclist patrols which had gone out far in advance of its Corps was surrounded near Roulers, and it was only by its capture that the enemy definitely discovered the arrival of the new German Corps, whose formation, however, had not been unknown to him, thanks to his good Secret Service system. Field-Marshal French was now confronted with a new situation. The preparations for his big attack were not yet completed. The superiority of the masses already concentrated did not yet appear to him to be suffi-

---

[1] *The British Cavalry Corps (there was only one, the number is superfluous and suggests there were more) did not extend as far as Gheluvelt: its left was on the Ypres–Comines canal near Houthem.*

[2] *The I Corps did not reach Bixschoote on 18th October : its leading Division, the 2nd, did not reach the area Poperinghe–Boeschepe till 19th October : the 1st Division was still detraining in the Hazebrouck area on 18th October.*

[3] *'Armée' in the original, but this is no doubt a misprint.*

cient to guarantee success against the enemy's advance. The British commander therefore decided to remain on the defensive [1] against our new Fourth Army, until the completion of the French concentration. His line was already closed up to the sea, it was naturally strong, and fresh troops were arriving daily. The danger threatening Dunkirk and Calais had the effect of making England put forth her full energy; the British troops fought desperately to defend every inch of ground, using every possible means to keep up the sinking spirits of the Belgians. They demanded and received rapid assistance from the French, and were backed up by fresh reinforcements from England.

From the German point of view the patriotic enthusiasm and unconditional determination to win the war which pervaded the new Fourth Army gave every prospect of successfully closing with the enemy, who was apparently still engaged in concentrating and reorganising his forces, and gaining Calais, the aim and object of the 1914 campaign.

Our offensive, however, struck against a powerful army, fully deployed and ready to meet us. The British boast that they held up our attack with a great inferiority of numbers, but this was only true in the case of the 7th Division during the first two days in the small sector ZONNEBEKE–GHELUVELT. On 22nd October between ARMENTIÈRES and the sea there were eight Corps opposed to the seven attacking German Corps; and, besides, the enemy had prepared a series of lines of strong trenches covered by

---

[1] *This statement as to Sir J. French's intentions is inaccurate. The II and III Corps were ordered to stand on the defensive, but the orders issued to the I Corps on 20th October were for an attack.*

an extensive system of artificial obstacles. In the course of the operations that developed, the relative strength of the opposing forces never appreciably altered in our favour.[1] The moral strength of our troops made up for the numerical superiority of the enemy. Our attack drove the hostile lines well back and destroyed, it is hoped for ever, the ambition of our opponent to regain Belgium by force of arms.

The great desire of the Germans to defeat the hostile northern wing, and to hit hardest the most hated of all our enemies, and, on the other side, the obstinate determination of the British to hold on to the passages to their country, and to carry out the offensive to the Rhine with all their resources, resulted in this battle being one of the most severe of the whole war. The deeds of our troops, old and young, in the battle on the YSER and of YPRES can never be sufficiently praised, and in spite of great losses their enthusiasm remained unchecked and their offensive spirit unbroken.

---

[1] *Between Armentières and the sea the British had only the I Corps, less than half the III Corps, the Cavalry Corps, the IV Corps (composed of one Division only), the French had a weak Cavalry Corps and two Territorial Divisions, the six Belgian Divisions were reduced to about one half of their establishment, so that the claim that the Allied forces outnumbered the Germans is hardly tenable. The value of the statement that 'the relative strength of the opposing forces never appreciably altered in our favour' will become apparent as the book is read, and as it is shown that the same British units, reinforced only by a weak composite Division drawn from the II Corps, were attacked by a succession of fresh German Corps, that the same units who repulsed the attacks at Langemarck on 23rd October, were in line at Gheluvelt on 31st October when the Prussian Guard attacked on 11th November. See also Introduction.*

THE THEATRE OF OPERATIONS

THE country in which it was hoped to bring about the final decision of the campaign of 1914 was not favourable to an attack from east to west.

Western Flanders, the most western part of Belgium, is almost completely flat, and lies only slightly above sea-level, and in some parts is even below it. Mount KEMMEL, in the south, is the only exception; rising to a height of over 500 feet, it is the watch-tower of Western Flanders. Before the war it was a well-wooded ridge with pretty enclosures and villages. From its slopes and summits could be seen the whole countryside from LILLE to MENIN and DIXMUDE.

The possession of this hill was of great importance. Our cavalry actually occupied it during the early days of October, but when the enemy advanced he immediately attacked it. The XIX Saxon Corps was still too far away to help, and so Mount KEMMEL fell into the enemy's hands. During the battle of YPRES it was his best observation post, and of the utmost assistance to his artillery.

We repeatedly succeeded in gaining a footing on the eastern crest of the ridge in front of YPRES, but in the autumn of 1914, as also later in the war, this was always the signal for the most desperate fighting.

It was thus that the heights of ST. ELOI,[1] the high-lying buildings of HOOGE and the village of WYTSCHAETE won their sanguinary fame.

Lying in the midst of luxuriant meadows, with its high ramparts and fine buildings, YPRES was formerly one of the most picturesque towns in Flanders. In the fourteenth century it had a considerable importance, and became the centre of the cloth-weaving trade on its introduction from Italy. BRUGES, lying close to the coast, became the market for its wares. The Clothweavers' Guild, which accumulated great wealth, erected in YPRES a fine Gothic hall, whose towers with those of St. Martin's Church were landmarks for miles round. In modern times, however, the importance of the town greatly diminished. The cloth-weaving industry drifted away to the factories of MENIN and COURTRAI ; and YPRES, like its dead neighbour BRUGES, remained only a half-forgotten memory of its former brilliance.

The war has brought fresh importance to the town, but of a mournful kind. On the impact of the German and Anglo-French masses in Flanders in the autumn of 1914, it became the central pivot of the operations. The enemy dug his heels into the high ground in front of it ; for, as an Englishman has written, it had become a point of honour to hold the town. YPRES lay so close to the front that our advance could be seen from its towers, and the enemy was able to use it for concealing his batteries and sheltering his reserves. For the sake of our troops we had to bring it under fire ;

---

[1] *'The heights of St. Eloi' is a phrase which suggests that the author cannot have visited the ground nor studied a contoured map of the area round Ypres.*

for German life is more precious than the finest Gothic architecture. Thus the mythical death of YPRES became a reality : no tower now sends forth its light across the countryside, and a wilderness of wrecked and burnt-out houses replaces the pretty town so full of legend and tradition in the history of Flanders.

The streams which run northwards from the hills about YPRES unite for the most part near the town and flow into the YSER canal, which connects the LYS at COMINES with the sea at NIEUPORT. This canal passes through the YPRES ridge near HOLLEBEKE and, following northwards the course of a small canalised tributary of the YSER, meets the YSER itself south of DIXMUDE. The dunes at NIEUPORT have been cut through by engineers for its exit to the sea. It is only from DIXMUDE northwards that the canal becomes an obstacle which requires proper bridging equipment for its passage. Its high embankments to the south of DIXMUDE, however, give excellent cover in the otherwise flat country and greatly simplify the task of the defender.

The canal acquired a decisive importance when the hard-pressed Belgians, during the battle on the night of 29th-30th October, let in the sea at flood-tide through the sluices into the canal, and then by blowing up the sluice-gates at NIEUPORT, allowed it to flood the battlefield along the lower YSER. By this means they succeeded in placing broad stretches of country under water, so much so that any extensive military operations in that district became out of the question. The high water-level greatly influenced all movements over a very large area. By his order the King of the Belgians destroyed for years the natural wealth of a considerable part of his fertile country, for the sea-water must have ruined all vegetation down to its very roots.

The country on both sides of the canal is flat, and difficult for observation purposes. The high level of the water necessitates drainage of the meadows, which for this purpose are intersected by deep dykes which have muddy bottoms. The banks of the dykes are bordered with willows, and thick-set hedges form the boundaries of the cultivated areas. Generally speaking, the villages do not consist of groups of houses: the farms are dispersed either singly, or in rows forming a single street. The country is densely populated and is consequently well provided with roads. But these are only good where they have been made on embankments and are paved. The frequent rains, which begin towards the end of October, rapidly turn the other roads into mere mud tracks and in many cases make them quite useless for long columns of traffic.

The digging of trenches was greatly complicated by rain and surface-water. The loam soil was on the whole easy to work in; but it was only on the high ground that trenches could be dug deep enough to give sufficient cover against the enemy's artillery fire; on the flat, low-lying ground they could not in many cases be made more than two feet deep.

A few miles south of the coast the country assumes quite another character: there are no more hedges and canals: instead gently rolling sand-hills separate the land from the sea, and this deposited sand is not fertile like the plains south of them. A belt of dunes prevents the sea encroaching on the land.

The greatest trouble of the attacker in all parts of Flanders is the difficulty of observation. The enemy, fighting in his own country,[1] had every advantage, while our artillery observation posts were only found with the utmost trouble. Our fire had to be directed from the front line, and it frequently happened that our brave artillerymen had to bring up their guns into the front infantry lines in order to use them effectively. Although the enemy was able to range extremely accurately on our guns which were thus quickly disclosed, nothing could prevent the German gunners from following the attacking infantry.

Observation from aeroplanes was made very difficult by the many hedges and villages, so that it took a long time to discover the enemy's dispositions and give our artillery good targets.

Finally, the flat nature of the country and the consequent limitations of view were all to the advantage of the defenders, who were everywhere able to surprise the attackers. Our troops were always finding fresh defensive lines in front of them without knowing whether they were occupied or not. The British, many of whom had fought in a colonial war against the most cunning of enemies in equally difficult country, allowed the attacker to come to close quarters and then opened a devastating fire at point-blank range from rifles and machine-guns concealed in houses and trees.

In many cases the hedges and dykes split up the German attacks so that even the biggest operations degenerated into disconnected actions which made the

---

[1] *The British and French in Belgium were hardly in their own country.*

greatest demands on the powers of endurance and individual skill of our volunteers. In spite of all these difficulties our men, both old and young, even when left to act on their own initiative, showed a spirit of heroism and self-sacrifice which makes the battle on the YSER a sacred memory both for the Army and the Nation, and every one who took part in it may say with pride, ' I was there.'

THE ADVANCE OF THE FOURTH ARMY

An Army Order of 16th October 1914 gave the following instructions for the 18th :—

> The III Reserve Corps to march to the line COXYDE–FURNES–OEREN, west of the YSER.
>
> The XXII Reserve Corps to the line AERTRYCKE–THOUROUT.
>
> The XXIII Reserve Corps to the line LICHTERVELDE–ARDOYE.
>
> The XXVI Reserve Corps to the Area EMELGHEM–ISEGHEM, and, on the left wing, the XXVII Reserve Corps to the line LENDELEDE–COURTRAI.

The XXII, XXIII, XXVI and XXVII Reserve Corps all reached their appointed destinations on the evening of the 18th without meeting any strong resistance. Along almost the whole front our advanced guards and patrols came into touch with weak hostile detachments who were awaiting our advance well entrenched, and surprised us with infantry and artillery fire. At ROULERS a hot skirmish took place. Aeroplanes circling round, motor-lorries bustling about, and cavalry patrols pushing well forward showed that the British now realised the strength of the new German forces.

In the meantime, on the extreme right wing of the

DISPOSITIONS ON OCTOBER 20TH 1914.

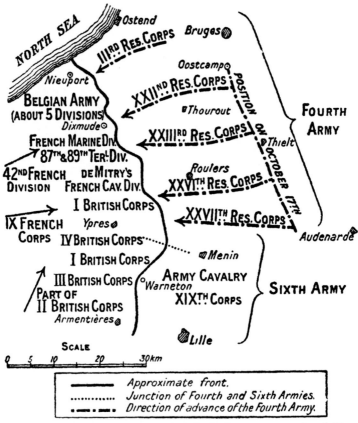

On 20th October none of the I British Corps were on the right
of the IV Corps : the map should read British Cavalry Corps.
It is also inaccurate to represent the whole III British Corps
as north of Armentières—only one of its Divisions was—
while the II Corps was certainly too closely pressed to detach
any troops to the north as depicted in the diagram.

Army, the troops of General von Beseler had opened the battle on the YSER. During its advance northwards to cross the Yser at the appointed places the III Reserve Corps had encountered strong opposition east of the river-barrier. The men knew they were on the decisive wing of the attack, and they pushed ahead everywhere regardless of loss. In a rapid assault the 4th *Ersatz* Division captured WESTENDE from the Belgians, although a gallant defence was put up, and in spite of the fact that British torpedo-boats and cruisers took part in the action from the sea with their heavy artillery [1] both during the advance and the fight for the town. Further south the 5th Reserve Division deployed to attack a strongly entrenched hostile position. The 3rd Reserve *Jäger* Battalion captured the obstinately defended village of ST. PIERRE CAPPELLE after severe hand-to-hand fighting, whilst the main body of the division succeeded in pushing forward to the neighbourhood of SCHOORE. The 6th Reserve Division, commanded by General von Neudorff, also closed with the enemy. It captured LEKE, and KEYEM, defended by the 4th Belgian Division; but even this Brandenburg Division, for all its war experience, found the task of forcing the crossings over the YSER too much for it.

The fighting on 18th October resulted in bringing us a thousand or two thousand yards nearer the YSER, but it had shown that the fight for the river line was to be a severe one. The Belgians seemed determined to sell the last acres of their kingdom only at the highest possible price. Four lines of trenches had been dug, and it could be seen that every modern

---

[1] *British torpedo boats do not carry ' heavy artillery.'*

scientific resource had been employed in putting the villages on the eastern bank of the river into a state of defence. A great number of guns, very skilfully placed and concealed, shelled the ground for a considerable distance east of the river, and in addition to this our right flank was enfiladed by the heavy naval guns from the sea. Battleships, cruisers and torpedo-boats worried the rear and flank of the 4th *Ersatz* Division with their fire, and the British had even brought heavy artillery on flat-bottomed boats close inshore.[1] They used a great quantity of ammunition, but the effect of it all was only slight, for the fire of the naval guns was much dispersed and indicated bad observation. It became still more erratic when our long-range guns were brought into action against the British Fleet. Detachments of the 4th *Ersatz* Division had to be echeloned back as far as Ostend, in order to defend the coast against hostile landings. During the day the General Commanding the III Reserve Corps decided not to allow the 4th *Ersatz* Division to cross the YSER at NIEUPORT, on account of the heavy fire from the British naval guns, but to make it pass with the main body of the Corps behind the 5th Reserve Division in whose area the fight appeared to be progressing favourably. The *Ersatz* Division was informed accordingly. On the 19th another effort would have to be made to force the crossings of the river by frontal attack, for everywhere to the south strong opposition had been encountered. From near DIXMUDE French troops carried on the line of the compact Belgian Army. It was

---

[1] *The vessels described as flat-bottomed boats were presumably the Monitors ' Severn,' ' Humber,' and ' Mersey.'*

against these that the new Reserve Corps were now advancing.

On the night of the 18th and morning of the 19th October a strong attack was delivered from the west by the 4th Belgian Division, and from the south-west by a brigade of the 5th Belgian Division and a brigade of French Marine Fusiliers under Admiral Ronarch, against KEYEM, held by part of the 6th Reserve Division. They were driven back after heavy fighting. During the 19th the southern wing of the Brandenburg (III) Reserve Corps succeeded in advancing nearer the river and, on its left, part of the artillery of the XXII Reserve Corps came into action in support of it, thereby partly relieving the III Reserve Corps, which until that day had been fighting unassisted.

On the 19th more or less heavy fighting developed on the whole front of the Fourth Army. The XXII Reserve Corps advanced on BEERST and DIXMUDE and fought its way up into line with the III Reserve Corps. In front of it lay the strong bridge-head of DIXMUDE, well provided with heavy guns. The whole XXIII Reserve Corps had to be deployed into battle-formation, as every locality was obstinately defended by the enemy. In the advance of the 45th Reserve Division the 209th Reserve Regiment late in the evening took HANDZAEME after severe street fighting, and the 212th Reserve Regiment took the village of GITS, whilst CORTEMARCK was evacuated by the enemy during the attack. The 46th Reserve Division in a running fight crossed the main road to THOUROUT, north of ROULERS, and by the evening had arrived close to STADEN. Heavy street fighting in the latter place continued during the night : the

enemy, supported by the population, offered strong
resistance in every house, so that isolated actions continued behind our front lines, endangering the cohesion
of the attacking troops, but never to a serious extent.

The XXVI Reserve Corps encountered strong opposition at RUMBEKE, south-east of ROULERS ; but all
the enemy's efforts were in vain, and the 233rd Reserve
Infantry Regiment, under the eyes of its Corps Commander, General von Hügel, forced its way through
the rows of houses, many of which were defended with
light artillery and machine-guns. A very heavy fight
took place for the possession of ROULERS, which was
stubbornly defended by the French ; barricades were
put up across the streets, machine-guns fired from
holes in the roofs and windows, and concealed mines
exploded among the advancing troops. In spite of
all this, by 5 P.M. ROULERS was taken by the 233rd,
234th and 235th Reserve Infantry Regiments, attacking from north, east and south respectively. Further
to the south, after a small skirmish with British cavalry,
the 52nd Reserve Division reached MORSLEDE, its
objective for the day. On its left again, the XXVII
Reserve Corps had come into contact with the 3rd
British Cavalry Division which tried to hold up the
Corps in an advanced position at ROLLEGHEM-CAPPELLE.
After a lively encounter the British cavalry was
thrown back on to the 7th British Division, which
held a strong position about DADIZEELE.[1]

---

[1] *This narrative omits the advance of the 7th Division on Menin,
19th October, which was going well when it had to be suspended on
account of the threatening advance of strong German columns from the
eastward.   The division was skilfully extricated and fell back to the line
Kruseik–Noordwesthoek–Broodseinde–Zonnebeke, the Germans failing
to press their pursuit.*

Thus by the evening of 19th October the situation had been considerably cleared up, in so far as we now knew that the Belgians, French and British not only held the YSER and the YPRES canal, but also the high ground east and north-east of YPRES. Everything pointed to the fact that an unexpectedly strong opponent was awaiting us in this difficult country, and that a very arduous task confronted the comparatively untrained troops of Duke Albert of Würtemburg's Army. In the meantime the Commander of the Sixth Army, Crown Prince Rupert of Bavaria, after a discussion at Army Headquarters with General von Falkenhayn, Chief of the General Staff, decided to renew the attack, as the left wing of the Fourth Army had now come up on his immediate right. In consequence of this decision, the XIII Corps was moved from its position on the line MENIN–WARNETON and replaced by three Cavalry Divisions of the IV Cavalry Corps. There can be no doubt that the attacks of the Sixth Army, which began on the 20th and were continued with frequent reinforcements of fresh troops, had the effect of holding the enemy and drawing a strong force to meet them. They were not, however, destined to have any decisive success, for the offensive strength of the Sixth Army had been reduced by previous fighting, and it was not sufficient to break through the enemy's strongly entrenched positions.[1] All the more therefore were the hopes of Germany centred in the Fourth Army, which was fighting further northwards, for in its hands lay the fate of the campaign in Western Europe at this period.

---

[1] *The constant exaggeration by this narrative of the strength of very hastily constructed British trenches is a noteworthy feature.*

THE OPERATIONS OF THE FOURTH ARMY
FROM 20TH OCTOBER TO 31ST OCTOBER 1914

ON 20th October the battle broke out along the whole line, on a front of about sixty miles. The enemy had got into position, and was prepared to meet the attack of Duke Albert of Würtemburg's Army. On the very day that the British, French and Belgians intended to begin their advance they found themselves compelled to exert all their strength to maintain their positions against our offensive. The British and French had to bring up constant reinforcements, and a hard and bitter struggle began for every yard of ground. The spirit in which our opponents were fighting is reflected in an order of the 4th Belgian Division, picked up in PERVYSE on 16th October. This ran: 'The fate of the whole campaign probably depends on our resistance. I (General Michel) implore officers and men, notwithstanding what efforts they may be called upon to make, to do even more than their mere duty. The salvation of the country and therefore of each individual among us depends on it. Let us then resist to our utmost.'

We shall see how far the soldiers of the Fourth Army, opposed to such a determined and numerically superior enemy, were able to justify the confidence which had been placed in them, a confidence expressed in the following proclamations by their highest commanders on their arrival in Belgium:

GREAT HEADQUARTERS,
14th October 1914.

To THE FOURTH ARMY,—I offer my welcome to the Fourth Army, and especially to its newly-formed Reserve Corps, and I am confident that these troops will act with the same devotion and bravery as the rest of the German Army.

Advance, with the help of God—my watchword.

(Signed) WILLIAM, I. R.

ARMY ORDER.

I am pleased to take over the command of the Army entrusted to me by the Emperor. I am fully confident that the Corps which have been called upon to bring about the final decision in this theatre of war will do their duty to their last breath with the old German spirit of courage and trust, and that every officer and every man is ready to give his last drop of blood for the just and sacred cause of our Fatherland. With God's assistance victory will then crown our efforts.

Up and at the enemy.   Hurrah for the Emperor.

(Signed) DUKE ALBERT OF WÜRTEMBURG,
General and Army Commander.

ARMY HEADQUARTERS, BRUSSELS,
15th October 1914.

Who can deny that the task set to the Fourth Army was not an infinitely difficult one. It would have probably been achieved nevertheless if the Belgians at the moment of their greatest peril had not called the sea to their aid to bring the German attack to a halt. Let us, however, now get down to the facts.

On 20th October the III Reserve Corps, the battering ram of the Fourth Army, began an attack with its 5th Reserve Division, supported by almost the whole of the Corps artillery, against the sector of the Yser west of the line MANNEKENSVERE–SCHOOR-

BAKKE. The 4th *Ersatz* Division to the north and the 6th Reserve Division to the south co-operated. By the early hours of the 22nd, the 5th and 6th Reserve Divisions had driven the enemy back across the river in spite of the support given him by British and French heavy batteries.[1] In front of the 4th *Ersatz* Division the enemy still held a bridge-head at LOMBARTZYDE. At 8.15 A.M. on the 22nd the glad tidings reached the Staff of the 6th Reserve Division, that part of the 26th Reserve Infantry Regiment had crossed the YSER. Under cover of darkness the 1st and 2nd Battalions of this regiment had worked their way up to the north-eastern part of the bend of the YSER, south of SCHOORE, and had got into the enemy's outposts on the eastern bank with the bayonet. Not a shot had been fired, and not an unnecessary noise had disturbed the quiet of the dawning day. Volunteers from the engineers silently and rapidly laid bridging material over the canal. In addition an old footbridge west of KEYEM, which had been blown up and lay in the water, was very quickly made serviceable again with some planks and baulks. The Belgians had considered their position sufficiently protected by the river, and by the outposts along the eastern bank. By 6 A.M. German patrols were on the far side of the YSER, and the enemy's infantry and machine-gun fire began only when they started to make a further advance. Three companies of the 1st and two companies of the 2nd Battalion, however, as well as part of the 24th Reserve Infantry Regiment, had already crossed the temporary bridges at the double and taken

---

[1] *There were no British heavy batteries in this quarter, unless it is to the guns of Rear-Admiral Hood's squadron that reference is made.*

up a position on the western bank : so that, in all, 2½ battalions and a machine-gun company were now on the western bank.

The enemy realised the seriousness of the situation, and prepared a thoroughly unpleasant day for those who had crossed. Heavy and light guns of the British and French artillery [1] hammered incessantly against the narrow German bridge-head and the bridges to it. Lying without cover in the swampy meadows the infantry was exposed beyond all help to the enemy's rifle and machine-gun fire from west and south-west. The small force repulsed counter-attacks again and again, but to attempt sending reinforcements across to it was hopeless. Some gallant gunners, however, who had brought their guns close up to the eastern bank, were able to give great help to their friends in their critical situation. Thus assisted the infantry succeeded in holding the position, and during the following night was able to make it sufficiently strong to afford very small prospect of success to any further hostile efforts. During the night several Belgian attacks with strong forces were repulsed with heavy loss, and the 6th Reserve Division was able to put a further 2½ battalions across to the western bank of the YSER bend. On the 23rd we gained possession of TERVAETE, and the dangerous enfilade fire on our new positions was thereby considerably diminished. Dawn on 24th October saw all the infantry of the 6th Reserve Division west of the river. A pontoon bridge was thrown across the north-eastern part of the YSER bend, but it was still impossible to bring guns forward on account

---

[1] *There was no British artillery present in this quarter.*

of the enemy's heavy artillery fire. The 5th Reserve Division still lay in its battle positions along the river bank north of SCHOORBAKKE, but every time attempts were made to cross the French and Belgian artillery smashed the bridges to pieces. The 4th *Ersatz* Division suffered heavily, as it was subjected to constant artillery fire from three sides, and to entrench was hopeless on account of the shifting sands and the high level of the ground water. Whenever fire ceased during the night strong hostile attacks soon followed; but they were all repulsed. The withdrawal of the main body of the *Ersatz* Division behind the 6th Reserve Division to cross the YSER, as General von Beseler had once planned, had become impracticable for the moment, for it had been discovered through the statements of prisoners that the 42nd French Division had arrived in NIEUPORT to assist the Belgians. The 4th *Ersatz* Division, which had been weakened on the 18th by the transfer of one of its three brigades to the 5th Reserve Division, could not be expected to bring the new enemy to his knees by the running fight that it had been hitherto conducting. The canal alone was sufficient obstacle to make this impracticable; in addition, the fire of the enemy's naval guns from the sea prevented any large offensive operations in the area in question. Thus the *Ersatz* troops were compelled to resign themselves to the weary task of maintaining their positions under the cross-fire of guns of every calibre, to driving back the hostile attacks, and to holding the Belgian and French forces off in front of them by continually threatening to take the offensive. It was not until some long-range batteries were placed at the disposal of the division that its

position improved. A couple of direct hits on the
enemy's ships soon taught them that they could no
longer carry on their good work undisturbed. Their
activity at once noticeably decreased, and the more
the German coast-guns gave tongue seawards from
the dunes, the further the ships moved away from
the coast and the less were they seen.

General von Beseler never for a moment doubted
that the decision lay with the 5th and 6th Reserve
Divisions, especially as the four Corps of the Fourth
Army, fighting further south, had not yet been able
to reach the canal-barrier with any considerable forces.

The XXII Reserve Corps, commanded by General
of Cavalry von Falkenhayn, had in the meantime
come into line south of General von Beseler's troops,
and had already fought some successful actions. It
had arrived on the 19th in the district east of BEERST
and about VLADSLOO, just in time to help in driving
back the Franco-Belgian attack against the southern
flank of the 6th Reserve Division.* That same evening it was ordered to attack from north and south
against the DIXMUDE bridge-head, an exceptionally
difficult task. In addition to the fact that the
swampy meadows of the YSER canal limited freedom
of movement to an enormous extent, the HAND-
ZAEME canal, running at right angles to it from east
to west, formed a most difficult obstacle. DIX-
MUDE lay at the junction of these two waterways,
and behind its bridge-head lines were the Belgian
' Iron ' Brigade under Colonel Meiser, the French
Marine Fusilier Brigade under Admiral Ronarch, and
part of the 5th Belgian Division, determined to defend

---

* See pages 23-24.

the place at all costs. About eighty guns of every calibre commanded with frontal and enfilade fire the ground over which Falkenhayn's Corps would have to attack. On the 20th, in spite of all these difficulties, the 44th Reserve Division, on the northern wing of the Corps, captured BEERST and reached the canal bank west of KASTEELHOEK in touch with von Beseler's Corps. The 43rd Reserve Division, advancing on the left wing, took VLADSLOO and several villages south-east of it on the northern bank of the HANDZAEME Canal. By the light of the conflagration of those villages the reach of the canal between EESSEN and ZARREN was crossed on hastily constructed foot-bridges, and a further advance made in a south-westerly direction. EESSEN itself was occupied, and the attack brought us to within a hundred yards of the enemy. He realised his extremely critical situation,* and his cyclists and all possible reserves at hand were put in to the fight. Owing to the severe hostile artillery fire the German losses were by no means slight. On one occasion when our advancing infantry units were losing touch with one another in this difficult country, a big hostile counter-attack was delivered from DIXMUDE. After a heavy struggle the onrush of the enemy was held up, mainly owing to our artillery, which heroically brought its guns up into position immediately behind the infantry front line.

During the night the 43rd Reserve Division re-organised in order to recommence its attack on the bridge-head from east and south-east on the following morning. Days of terrific fighting ensued. The garrison of the bridge-head had received orders to

---

* See *Les pages de gloire de l'Armée Belge : à Dixmuide.*

hold out to the last man, and had been informed that any one who attempted to desert would be shot without mercy by men placed for this purpose to guard all the exits from the town. The Belgians were indeed fighting for their very existence as a nation. Nevertheless by the 21st October the 43rd Reserve Division, which consisted of volunteers from the Guard Corps Reservists, had taken the château south of DIXMUDE, and WOUMEN. The opposing sides lay within a hundred yards of each other. Artillery preparation, attack and counter-attack went on incessantly. Our artillery did fearful havoc and DIXMUDE was in flames. The Franco-Belgian garrison was, however, constantly reinforced, and conducted itself most gallantly. From the north the battalions of the 44th Reserve Division were able to advance slightly and drive the enemy back on to the town, and German batteries were brought up into, and at times even in front of, the infantry front line. Although we were unable to force our way into DIXMUDE, on the evening of the 23rd our troops were in position all round it.

On the left of the XXII Reserve Corps, the XXIII Reserve Corps, under General of Cavalry von Kleist, had advanced at 9 A.M. on 20th October on the front HANDZAEME–STADEN in order to reach the canal on the line NOORDSCHOOTE–BIXSCHOOTE. The 45th Reserve Division was on the right and the 46th Reserve Division on the left. After some hours of street fighting STADEN was finally surrounded and taken by the 46th Reserve Division. By nightfall a line from CLERCKEN to the eastern edge of HOUTHULST Forest was reached. On the 21st the Corps had to cross a stretch of country which put these partially trained troops and their

C

inexperienced officers to a very severe test. The great forest of HOUTHULST with its dense undergrowth made it exceedingly difficult to keep direction in the attack and to maintain communication between units fighting an invisible opponent. Small swampy streams such as the STEENEBECK offered favourable opportunities to the enemy to put up a strong defence behind a succession of depressions. Thus our gallant troops after every successful assault found themselves confronted by another strong position : but unwavering and regardless of loss, they continued their advance.

By the evening of the 21st the 46th Reserve Division had completely driven the enemy out of HOUT-HULST Forest,[1] whilst its sister-division had advanced north of the STEENEBECK, and with its northern wing supporting the Corps fighting immediately north of it, had pushed forward to beyond WOUMEN. On the morning of the 22nd the heavy artillery opened fire against the French positions on the YSER canal to prepare the break-through. Unfortunately however only the northern Division was able to reach the sector allotted to the Corps, and an Army Order directed the 46th Reserve Division to the south-west against the line BIXSCHOOTE–LANGEMARCK, in order to help carry for-

---

[1] *The narrative omits to state precisely the nature of the opposition which was encountered in the Houthulst area. Actually the Allied force in this quarter merely consisted of General de Mitry's French Cavalry Corps and a few battalions of French Cyclists and Territorials. These were driven back without being able to offer much resistance, and in consequence uncovered the flank of the I British Corps just as it began its advance north-east of Ypres on Poelcapelle and Passchendaele (21st October). This forced Sir Douglas Haig to divert his reserves to protect his left flank, and therefore to suspend his attack which had been making good progress on a line south-east from Langemarck to Zonnebeke, where he linked up with the left of the 7th Division.*

ward the attack of the XXVI Reserve Corps, which
was completely held up in front of the latter place. As
a result of this the advance of von Kleist's Corps also
came to a standstill, although it had achieved considerable fame during the day. In spite of a desperate
resistance the 210th Reserve Regiment stormed the
strongly entrenched village of MERCKEM and the village
of LUYGHEM lying north of it ; a daring attack by the
209th and 212th Reserve Regiments broke through
the enemy's positions on the MURTJE VAART, whilst
the 46th Reserve Division attempted to overrun the
KORTEBECK sector, supported by the concentrated
fire of its artillery in position along the south-western
edge of HOUTHULST Forest. The 216th Reserve Regiment took MANGELAERE by storm, in doing which its
gallant commander, Colonel von Grothe, was killed
at the head of his troops. The 1st British Division
held a strong position along the KORTEBECK, in touch
with the French, and artillery of every calibre near
NOORDSCHOOTE enfiladed the German attack.[1] The
British themselves speak of our attack as a magni-

---

[1] *By no means the whole of the 1st British Division was holding the
line of the Kortebeck. From Steenstraate, which was held by the 1st
Scots Guards, who were never seriously pressed on 22nd October, the
1st Cameron Highlanders were extended over a wide front nearly to
Langemarck, where the 1st Coldstream Guards connected them up with
the 3rd Infantry Brigade (1st Queen's, 1st S.W.B., 1st Gloucesters, and
2nd Welsh) which was holding a position north and north-east of Langemarck. The rest of the infantry of the 1st Division was in reserve,
and only one 18-pounder battery (46th Batty. R.F.A.) was available
to support the Camerons. On the right of the 3rd Infantry Brigade the
2nd Division carried on the line south-east to Zonnebeke with the 5th
Infantry Brigade on its left and the 4th (Guards) Brigade on its right.
This division was about on the line of the Zonnebeke–Langemarck road :
it repulsed several counter-attacks on the afternoon of 21st October and
night 21st-22nd.*

ficent feat of arms carried out with infinite courage
and brilliant discipline. The men sang songs as they
charged through a hail of bullets in closed ranks up
to the enemy's defences. The 212th Reserve Regiment under Colonel Basedow, reinforced and carried
forward by fresh detachments of the 209th Reserve
Regiment, pushed its way into the strongly fortified
village of BIXSCHOOTE. The enemy on our side of
the canal, on the line BIXSCHOOTE–LANGEMARCK–
ZONNEBEKE, was threatened with annihilation. BIX-
SCHOOTE commanded the main road and the canal-
crossing to POPERINGHE, where the enemy was detraining his reinforcements.[1] The British therefore fought
with the courage of desperation : for not only was the
fate of the high ground east and north-east of YPRES
now in the balance, but also the chance of being able
to carry out the great Anglo-French offensive which
had been planned. YPRES and the high ground east
of the canal were on no account to be lost, and furious
counter-attacks were therefore delivered against the
intermingled German units. Nevertheless our gallant
volunteers pressed on, using their bayonets and the
butts of their rifles, until the furious hand-to-hand
fighting was finally decided in our favour. At 6.30
that evening BIXSCHOOTE was ours. Unfortunately,
however, owing to an order being misunderstood, it
was lost again during the night : the exhausted attacking troops were to be relieved under cover of darkness,
but they assembled and marched back before the
relieving force had arrived. The enemy, ever watchful,
immediately advanced into the evacuated village and

---

[1] *The British troops had not detrained at Poperinghe, but in the Hazebrouck area.*

took position among the ruins. Simultaneously a big hostile counter-attack drove the 46th Reserve Division from the high ground south of KORTEBECK, which it had captured, and pressed it back beyond the stream again. The spirit and strength of the young and inexperienced troops seemed to be broken, and only a few of the subordinate commanders had yet learnt how to deal with critical situations. Officers of the General Staff and Divisional Staffs had to help to reorganise the men ; they immediately turned and followed their new leaders, and were taken forward again to the attack. Thus on the 23rd the high ground south of the KORTEBECK was won back by the 46th Reserve Division, but BIXSCHOOTE remained lost to us, and LANGEMARCK could not be captured.[1]

---

[1] *This account is altogether at variance with the facts. On the after-noon of 22nd October the Germans at length succeeded in breaking through the thin and widely extended line of the 1st Cameron High-landers, and pushed them back south of the Langemarck–Bixschoote road, capturing the Kortekeer Cabaret. They failed to press forward ; however reinforcements, the 1st Northamptonshires and 1st Black Watch, arrived, and counter-attacks were made which checked all further German advance. Next morning (23rd October) further rein-forcements came up, the 1st Loyal North Lancashires and 2nd K.R.R.C. of the 2nd Infantry Brigade, part of the 2nd South Staffordshires from the 6th Infantry Brigade.· Finally, on the arrival of 1st Queen's of the 3rd Infantry Brigade, a most successful counter-attack was launched, the Queen's retook the Kortekeer Cabaret, and the Germans were driven right back, nearly 500 being taken and very heavy losses inflicted on them. The old trenches 800 yards north of the road were actually recovered, but late in the evening a fresh German attack recovered the advanced position reached by our counter-attack, and a new line was taken up about the line of the Langemarck–Bixschoote road. Meanwhile dur-ing this action, in which less than two British infantry brigades had defeated the 46th Reserve Division, the rest of the 1st Division at Lange-marck had been heavily attacked, apparently (cf. p. 40) by the 51st Reserve Division, which had been completely worsted. In this part of the action very notable service was done by two platoons of the Glou-*

On 22nd October, for the first time, our attack was
directed from the north against YPRES.   If the British
and French did not intend to give up their offensive
plans, and thereby their last hope of retaking Belgium
and the wealthy provinces of Northern France from
the hated German, they would have to maintain their
positions along the YPRES bridge-head east of the
canal between COMINES and the coast.   For this reason
the country round YPRES was the central area of the
Anglo-French defence from the beginning to the end
of the battle.   Our opponents defended this position
on a wide semicircle by successive lines of trenches
and with their best troops.   Every wood, every village,
every farm and even every large copse has won for
itself a fame of blood.   The reinforcements which
Field-Marshal French received in abundance he placed
round YPRES, but not only for defensive purposes ;
they were more often used to deliver attack after
attack against our young troops who had been weakened
by the hard fighting ; and on 23rd October they were
already being employed in this manner against the
46th Reserve Division.[1]   He hoped to use the oppor-

---

*cesters just north of Langemarck, who expended an average of 400
rounds a man, and though attacked in front and flank by very superior
numbers, maintained their position intact.   The British accounts
testify to the gallantry with which the German attacks were pressed,
officers carrying regimental colours ran on ahead of the men and
planted the colours in the ground to give their men a point to make for,
a mounted officer rode forward, exposing himself recklessly, to encourage his soldiers, but the musketry of the British infantry was too much
for the Germans, and the attack was completely repulsed.*

[1] *Throughout this narrative it is astonishing to read of the repeated
reinforcements which Sir John French received.   Actually, except for
a few drafts, no reinforcements joined the British in the Ypres salient
before the end of October : subsequently two Territorial battalions, the
Hertfordshires and the London Scottish, two Yeomanry regiments, the*

tunity of our retirement behind the KORTEBECK to
break through our line and to roll up the part of the
front lying to the north of it as far as the sea, and
thus to regain the initiative and freedom of manœuvre
on this extreme wing.[1] However, the blow was parried
by the 46th Reserve Division. In ragged, badly
placed lines the German units, which had scarcely
had time to reorganise, brought the hostile masses to
a standstill and won back in a counter-attack the
ground which they had lost during the night. On
this occasion, also, the gunners shared with the infantry the honours of the day. The fire of the guns,
brought up into the foremost lines, made wide gaps
in the attacking columns and the enemy's losses must
have been terrible. Our own troops had also suffered
severely in the constant fighting and under the ever-
lasting hostile artillery fire. Some of our regiments
had been reduced to half their strength. But in spite
of it the British did not succeed in breaking through
between the XXIII and XXVI Reserve Corps.

The XXVI and XXVII Reserve Corps were by this
time completely held up in front of strongly entrenched
positions on the line LANGEMARCK–ZONNEBEKE–GHELU-
VELT and opposed to an enemy who was becoming
stronger every day and making the most desperate

---

*North Somersets and the Leicestershires, and the 3rd Dragoon Guards,
the belated last unit of the 3rd Cavalry Division, were added to the force,
while the exhausted infantry of the 7th Division were replaced by three
composite brigades from the II Corps, set free after three weeks of
strenuous fighting near La Bassée by the arrival of the Meerut Division,
and greatly below strength.*

[1] *The British counter-attack at the Kortekeer Cabaret did not aim at
doing more than recover the ground lost on 22nd October : it was not
an attempt at break-through, and was quite successful in its immediate
object.*

efforts to regain his freedom of action and begin a
big offensive himself. The XXVI Reserve Corps,
which advanced on the morning of the 20th, the 51st
Reserve Division from the area west of ROULERS,
and the other Division from MORSLEDE, encountered
a stubborn resistance along the ridge WESTROOSE-
BEKE–PASSCHENDAELE–KEIBERG. Fighting under the
eyes of their general, who was himself in the thick of
the struggle, the 51st Reserve Division stormed the
slope on to the ridge and entered WESTROOSEBEKE.
The French division defending it was driven out at
four in the afternoon and, attacking incessantly, the
gallant 51st, supported by the 23rd Reserve *Jäger*
Battalion, reached a line from the railway-station
north-west of POELCAPPELLE to POELCAPPELLE itself
during the evening. The attack was all the more
daring through the fact that HOUTHULST Forest was
still in the enemy's hands, and the flank of the division
therefore appeared to be threatened. Meanwhile the
52nd Reserve Division had taken PASSCHENDAELE,
KEIBERG and the high ground between them from
the British ; the artillery again deserving the highest
praise for its co-operation.[1] The attack, however,

---

[1] *On 20th October the 7th Division held the line from Zandvoorde to
Kruiseik, thence to Broodseinde cross-roads east of Zonnebeke, the line
being continued by the 3rd Cavalry Division to Passchendaele. The
German 52nd Reserve Division and the XXVII Reserve Corps were
thus faced by less than half their numbers. Nevertheless the only effect
of their attack was that after the 51st Reserve Division had driven the
French out of Westroosebeke, the British Cavalry found its flank exposed
and had to retire on St. Julien, the 7th Division throwing back its left
flank to conform. There was no fighting for Keiberg, and the expulsion
of the 7th Division from Becelaere (mentioned nine lines below) after
heavy street fighting, seems to be based on the slender foundation that a
British reconnaissance was made in the direction of Gheluwe covered by*

was brought to a standstill in front of the enemy's main position at the cross-roads east of ZONNEBEKE. The XXVII Reserve Corps commanded by General von Carlowitz, formerly Saxon War Minister, lay in close touch with the 52nd Reserve Division on the evening of the 20th. Advancing in four columns and by constant fighting it had forced its way westwards. The Würtemburg Division had succeeded in driving the 7th British Division out of BECELAERE after heavy street fighting, and the left wing was bent back on TERHAND. Communication was there obtained with the 3rd Cavalry Division, fighting on the right wing of the Sixth Army, which had captured a hostile position north-east of KRUISEIK.

On the morning of the 22nd a strong position lay to our immediate front. It followed a line BIXSCHOOTE–LANGEMARCK–ZONNEBEKE–REUTEL–GHELUVELT ; and the I and IV British, as well as the IX French Corps,[1]

---

two battalions nearer Terhand, which fell back without being seriously pressed. The Germans advancing in the evening from Becelaere were sharply repulsed by the centre infantry brigade of the 7th Division east of Polygon Wood. The events of 21st–22nd October on the front from Langemarck to Kruiseik are somewhat slurred over in this narrative. Briefly, on 21st October the Germans pressed all along the line of the 7th Division without success except on the left, where by enfilade fire from Passchendaele they forced the left of the 22nd Infantry Brigade to fall back to the south-west of Zonnebeke. Meanwhile the advance of the I Corps relieved the pressure, and though, as already explained (see note, p. 34), the uncovering of the left of the I Corps prevented the advance being pressed beyond the line Zonnebeke–Langemarck, this line was made good and the German efforts to advance successfully repulsed. On 22nd October the Germans attacked the line of the 2nd Division north-west of Zonnebeke, but were easily repulsed, while further to their left they renewed their attacks on the 21st Infantry Brigade east of Polygon Wood with equal ill-success.

[1] *The IX French Corps was not yet up at the front. It did not begin relieving the 2nd Division till the afternoon of 23rd October.*

all picked troops, had already been located there.
They had dug a well-planned maze of trenches behind
broad wire entanglements before a single German shell
arrived to disturb their work.[1] The few stretches
of rising ground in the district had been included in
the skilfully selected positions as observation posts,
and the defenders were thus able to bring our advancing columns under accurate artillery fire at long range.
This was especially the case from the high ground near
ZONNEBEKE, whence the whole ground in front of
the position as far as LANGEMARCK could be enfiladed.
All these difficulties, however, were not sufficient to
deter the offensive spirit of the German troops, and
' Vorwärts' was still their watchword : forwards and
back with the enemy, so that the rigid western front
might once more be mobile. The main body of the
XXVI Reserve Corps attacked the fortress of LANGE-
MARCK [2] from north and east, whilst the XXVII
Reserve Corps fought for the upper hand in the woods
between ZONNEBEKE and BECELAERE. The great
efforts made by the artillery to follow up the infantry-
men with its guns and support them with their fire
were in vain, owing to the difficult country, and the
well-aimed fire from the enemy's prepared positions
reaped a big harvest. Leaders of all grades were

---

[1] *The ' well-planned maze of trenches behind broad wire entanglements ' would have been most welcome to the British.   Unfortunately
there had been no time or opportunity to do more than dig in hastily
where the advance of the I Corps had been checked, while such trenches
as the 7th Division had dug at Zonnebeke were hastily prepared in such
loose and sandy soil that they collapsed when bombarded ; wire was
conspicuous by its absence.*

[2] *The only thing in the nature of a ' fortress ' at Langemarck was a
small redoubt, built by the 26th Field Company R.E. on the night of
22nd-23rd October, and held by two platoons of the Gloucesters.*

killed, and officers of high rank took their places and reorganised the intermingled units.

With the failure of the 46th Reserve Division to gain a decisive victory between BIXSCHOOTE and LANGEMARCK on 22nd and 23rd October the fate of the XXVI and XXVII Reserve Corps was also settled. For the time being any further thought of a break-through was out of the question. The troops up till now had met the enemy full of a keen fighting spirit, and had stormed his positions singing ' *Deutschland, Deutschland über alles* ' regardless of casualties, and had been one and all ready to die for their country ; but they had suffered heavily in the contest against a war-experienced and numerically superior opponent entrenched in strongly fortified positions. Even when the last reserves of the Army, the 37th *Landwehr* Brigade and the 2nd *Ersatz* Brigade, had been placed at the disposal of the XXVI Reserve Corps, they could only be used to stiffen the defence. During the night of 23rd - 24th October the expected Anglo - French counter - attacks began, and continued throughout the 24th, against the front of the XXVI and the right wing of the XXVII Reserve Corps. By utilising tem-porary local successes and putting in fresh forces the enemy vainly hoped to prepare the way for a break-through ; but the German troops though weakened held up all these furious onslaughts from positions which had never been selected for defence, but were merely those reached at the close of the attack.[1]

---

[1] *This is hardly a recognisable account of what took place. The relief of the 1st Division by a French Territorial division did not take place till the night 24th-25th, but the 2nd Division was relieved by a division of the French IX Corps, and by the morning of 24th October it was concentrated at St. Jean in reserve. In the course of the morning*

The Commander of the Fourth Army was forced to continue ordering all his Corps to attack, in order to co-operate with the Sixth Army which was attacking and, besides this, to pin the enemy's forces opposed to him to their ground : for in the north a decision appeared to be imminent on the front of General von Beseler's III Reserve Corps : in addition to the entire infantry of the 6th Reserve Division, which had crossed the canal by the morning of 24th October, the infantry of the 5th Reserve Division and five battalions of the 44th Reserve Division succeeded in crossing the YSER during that day.   The enemy was compelled to evacuate the western bank of the canal from ST. GEORGE to south-east of STUYVEKENSKERKE, in spite of the fact that there had been one French and four Belgian Divisions [1] opposing the III Reserve Corps, and that the ten howitzer batteries had proved insufficient to engage the Belgian, French and British artillery successfully.   In consequence of this inferiority the old and new canal crossings lay under constant concentrated fire, and all our efforts to transport guns over the waterway failed.   Many a fine piece of engineering carried out by our indefatigable sappers

---

of 24th October the Reserve Division attacked the line of the 21st Infantry Brigade in overwhelming strength, and broke through north of Reutel, penetrating into Polygon Wood.   It was cleared out by a counter-attack by the 5th Infantry Brigade, 2nd Division, and the 2nd R. Warwicks of the 7th Division, and in the afternoon an advance was made north of Polygon Wood by the 6th Infantry Brigade in co-operation with the French IX Corps on the left.   Fair progress was made, the 6th Infantry Brigade crossing to the east of the Werwicq–Staden road. Further south the 7th Division held its own successfully and all attacks were repulsed.

[1] It has already been pointed out that the Belgian divisions were much below establishment.

was destroyed by the enemy's shells. The supply of ammunition and field-dressings became a matter of the greatest difficulty, as all the roads leading to the rear across the swampy meadows were continuously shelled for a long way back. Nevertheless our front troops held on firmly to their new positions. The next operation was to break through the enemy's position here once and for all, though it was clear from the beginning that the attack would be a very severe one. Belgian and French working parties had dug a series of positions between the YSER and the NIEU-PORT–BIXSCHOOTE railway, from which the ground in front could be commanded with frontal and enfilade fire from skilfully placed machine-guns and well-concealed batteries. On both wings, according to the latest information at hand, strong hostile attacks were threatening us, that is to say, near NIEUPORT as well as near and to the south of DIXMUDE. To meet these the Army Commander had replaced the 4th *Ersatz* Division, which had been echeloned back along the coast as a precaution against hostile landings, by detachments of the Marine Division, and a few troops placed at his disposition by the Governor of Belgium, and had ordered it to march to THOUROUT. At the same time, by order of General von Beseler, long-range guns were placed to prevent the enemy from concentrating for an attack in the NIEUPORT district. However, the expected attack took place in the neighbourhood of DIXMUDE, and was directed against those battalions of the 44th Reserve Division which had crossed to the west of the YSER. The enemy realised the great danger that threatened his bridge-head from the north-west, and put all available Belgian and

French reserves into the attack. Thus between five and six battalions from three Belgian regiments and the Marine Fusiliers under Admiral Ronarch, with a strong force of artillery, advanced to the attack of our southern flank. The Belgians themselves describe this attack in the following words : ' One saw the companies doubling forward in small groups, lying down on the officers' signal, and then getting up to go forward again until they finally deployed into their attacking lines. But unfortunately they were asked to accomplish a superhuman task, and whole rows of the men were mown down by the machine-guns. Company after company was decimated, and in spite of the energy of their leaders they had to give way, death having taken too heavy a toll of their ranks. The Marine Fusiliers, who attacked with uncommon gallantry, soon shared the same fate. But all this sacrifice was not in vain—it stopped the enemy's advance.' *

It will be understood then that the first thing for the weak and widely separated battalions of the 44th Reserve Division to do on the 25th was to get breathing space and reorganise, even though they were exposed all the time to the heaviest fire from west, south and south-east. Further to the north, however, on the morning of the 25th, the 5th and 6th Reserve Divisions had succeeded in bringing their field-batteries across the river, and as soon as the whole artillery of these two divisions had been concentrated under the expert leadership of General von Ziethen, it began to prepare the way for the infantry attack. By midday

---

* See *Les pages de gloire de l'Armée Belge : à Dixmuide.*

both the divisions were advancing steadily towards the railway embankment on the line RAMSCAPPELLE–PERVYSE. The Belgians had to evacuate position after position. Then suddenly heavy enfilade fire was poured in by the enemy's artillery about NIEU-PORT ; and simultaneously a brigade of the 6th Reserve Division south-east of PERVYSE had to be directed southwards in order not to lose touch with the right wing of the 44th Reserve Division. There were no reinforcements to fill up the gaps, and thus the attack came shortly afterwards to a standstill.

A very heavy thunder of guns rumbled incessantly from the south : the German artillery, including 42-centimetre guns, had bombarded DIXMUDE throughout the 24th October and morning of the 25th, and now the 43rd Reserve Division had begun its assault on the town. It resulted in the most violent street fighting ; fast and furious came the bullets from the machine-guns posted in the houses along the edge of the town, and from the shells from the batteries massed west of the YSER, but nothing could hold up our attack. The Belgians have given the following description of the power of the German assault : ' What plunder must not they have been promised, to allow themselves to be killed in such a way ? What drink must they not have taken to give themselves such animal courage ? Like devils, thirsting for blood, they storm forward with the howls of wild beasts ; lusting to massacre, they tread the wounded under foot and stumble over the dead : and, though shot down in hundreds, they keep coming on. Then follow isolated fights with bayonets and the butts of rifles : some are impaled, others strangled or have their skulls

bashed in.'   The fight swayed backwards and forwards
till well into the night : guns brought up into the
front line fired at point-blank range : both sides put
in their last reserves.

During the night, rifles were unloaded, bayonets
fixed, and we attacked again. A small German
detachment of about fifty men advanced across the
YSER bridge, but in endeavouring to assault the
enemy's batteries, it succumbed to greatly superior
numbers. Thus the morning of 26th October found
the attackers back in their assault-positions : their
courage, spirit and indifference to death having added
another leaf of fame to the chaplet of the Guards. It
was clear, however, that another artillery bombardment was indispensable to success, and it was carried
out on the 26th and 27th.

That heavy losses were suffered by the Belgians and
the French Marine Fusiliers in the fighting just described
is shown by the fact that on the morning of the 26th
Senegalese troops who had been hurriedly brought
up took over the defence of the bridge-head. A
German attack on the 28th was able to make some
progress on the southern flank against these fresh
troops, but a decision could not be obtained. No
further effort was made on the 29th, for there was a
shortage of artillery ammunition. The eastern edge
of the town was, however, bombarded by trench-
mortars, which had just arrived, with good effect.

Army Orders for the 30th prescribed that the XXII
Reserve Corps should only leave a weak force of from
three to four battalions on the eastern bank of the
YSER opposite DIXMUDE ; that DIXMUDE should be
kept under heavy artillery fire ; and that the remainder

of the 43rd Reserve Division should cross the YSER, north of DIXMUDE, in order to attack the town from the rear.

North-west of DIXMUDE, by the evening of the 29th, the troops of General von Beseler and the 44th Reserve Division had worked their way forward some 300 yards towards the railway embankment. Only one brigade of the 4th *Ersatz* Division was still north-east of NIEUPORT : all the rest were taking part in the struggle further south, and west of the YSER. NIEU-PORT was shut in on the south : the left wing of the 44th Reserve Division lay west of BEERST, as protection against the strong hostile forces near the river about DIXMUDE : the Belgians and recently-arrived French forces held the railway embankment between NIEUPORT and DIXMUDE. Broad stretches of wire entanglements lay in front of this strong position, and the efforts of our troops had been almost superhuman in their advance over this ground : it was intersected with patches of marsh, dykes often fifteen yards broad, and thick, wired hedges. So strong, however, was the pressure against the enemy that the French were compelled to reduce their forces about NIEUPORT and north of it to weak detachments, and send constant reinforcements to the area PERVYSE–RAMSCAPPELLE. A German airman, who was killed on the morning of the 30th, had shortly before his death reported that the enemy were beginning to withdraw. Our assault began at 6.30 A.M., though the ground in the area of the 5th and 6th Reserve Divisions had become extraordinarily swampy. It seemed impossible that the recent rains could have raised the level of the ground-water to such an extent. Nevertheless the attack

made considerable progress. The 11th Brigade of
the 6th Reserve Division succeeded in forcing its way
into the eastern part of the strongly-fortified village
of PERVYSE, whilst of the 5th Reserve Division, the
48th and 52nd Reserve Regiments reached the railway
embankment, and the 48th pushed on beyond it
towards RAMSCAPPELLE. Although every house had
to be attacked, it succeeded in reaching the western
end of the village. The 12th Reserve Regiment
also made considerable advance.

The resistance of the enemy was broken, and when
the 33rd *Ersatz* Brigade on the northern wing advanced
from the north-east against NIEUPORT, the enemy
retired. Airmen reported enemy's columns retreat-
ing towards FURNES. Nothing could stop the victorious advance of General von Beseler's troops, not
even the heaviest guns of the British battleships,
cruisers and torpedo-boats, which, from far out at sea,
enfiladed the German attack at a range of 20,000
yards, nor the incessant counter-attacks of the Franco-
Belgian Divisions. On the evening of the 30th RAMS-
CAPPELLE was completely in German possession, the
railway embankment south of it had been reached and
even crossed in places ; in PERVYSE the fight was
progressing favourably, and south of it the 12th
Reserve Brigade, delayed by the numerous broad
dykes, was working forward to the railway. Still
further south the 44th Reserve Division was in full
advance towards the railway embankment east of
OOSTKERKE, whilst the main body of the 43rd Reserve
Division had crossed the YSER, without casualties,
and had been sent forward in the direction of CAES-
KERKE.

The attack was to have been continued on the following morning, and General von Beseler intended to withdraw the last part of the 4th *Ersatz* Division, the 33rd *Ersatz* Brigade, from the area north-east of NIEUPORT, for the fire of the enemy's naval guns from the sea [1] and the difficulties of the country appeared to militate against any prospects of a rapid success there. At 11.30 P.M., however, a General Staff Officer of the 6th Reserve Division reported that the attack could be continued no further owing to the constant rising of the water. What had happened ? On the morning of the 30th the advancing troops had been up to their ankles in water ; then it had gradually risen until they were now wading up to their knees, and they could scarcely drag their feet out of the clayey soil. If any one lay down for a moment under the heavy artillery, machine-gun and rifle fire, he was lost. The rise of the waters was attributed to the torrential rain of the previous few days, and it was hoped that on the approach of dry weather the excellent system of canals would soon drain it off. But the rising flood soon prevented the movement of wagons with ammunition and supplies, and when the attackers looked back from the railway embankment, it seemed to them as if the whole country had sunk behind them : the green meadows were covered with dirty, yellow water, and the general line of the roads was only indicated by the houses and the rows of partly covered trees. It soon became evident that the enemy must have blown up the canal-

---

[1] *This testimony to the effective character of the help given by Admiral Hood's squadron is noteworthy, and contradicts what was said in the narrative on page 22.*

sluices, and called in the sea to his aid. The advance of General von Beseler's III Reserve Corps had been the culmination of the crisis for our opponent ; all his reserves had been put in to stop it, but in vain. If the Germans could only succeed in pushing the exhausted Belgians and French out of their way, the road to DUNKIRK and CALAIS was open. Warnings, friendly and otherwise, had been given by the Allies to the Belgians that they must ' hold out ' ; but they were no more able to resist the attacks of the victors of ANTWERP now than when behind fortress ramparts. Their fighting spirit was broken ; so, influenced by the wishes of the British and the French, King Albert finally decided to employ this last desperate means of defence, and place a wide expanse of his fair country under water. The water-level rose slowly and insidiously until, on the evening of the 30th, the YSER north of DIXMUDE had almost everywhere overflowed its banks. The inundation destroyed buildings as well as soil, but it enabled the worn-out defenders to recover their sore-threatened security.

General von Beseler quickly realised the danger which now awaited his attacking troops on the far side of the canal, behind whom a sheet of water, 2000 to 3000 yards broad, was constantly deepening. The decision was an exceedingly hard one for him to make, yet it had to be done. The attack would have to be given up and the greater part of the western bank of the river evacuated. The order was issued and carried out during the night of the 30th-31st October. In spite of the dangers due to the altered appearance of the country and the consequent difficulty in finding the way, and although the Franco-

Belgian artillery kept the YSER crossings under constant heavy fire, the withdrawal was a brilliant success. Not a wounded man nor rifle fell into the enemy's hands, and the movement was so well covered that the enemy did not notice we had disengaged until it was too late. A small detachment of gallant Brandenburgers under Lieutenant Buchholz remained behind for a long time in PERVYSE. In front of them the enemy was sweeping the village with artillery and infantry fire and behind them was the edge of an apparently boundless sea. A French colonel offered Lieutenant Buchholz honourable conditions if he would surrender ; but he indignantly rejected the offer : his only answer to the colonel was to slip off with his little band of followers. They rejoined their unit successfully. The enemy only followed up slowly along the roads, with weak detachments of infantry. Our rear-guards remained west of the canal on the line ST. GEORGE–STUYVEKENSKERKE, whilst the main body on the 31st took up its new position east of the YSER as follows : the 5th Reserve Division north of the main road ST. PIERRE CAPPELLE–MANNEKENSVERE; the 4th *Ersatz* Division in the area MANNEKENSVERE–SCHOORE ; and the 6th Reserve Division to the south of it. One battalion and one battery of the 4th *Ersatz* Division remained facing NIEUPORT, extending northwards to the coast. A new defensive position was selected along the line WESTENDE–MANNEKENSVERE–SCHOORE–KASTEELHOEK : a continuation of the attack was now out of the question, as the water was still rising west of the YSER. On 31st October and 1st November, however, the XXII Reserve Corps again tried to press its attack southwards on the east bank of the river, in order to isolate the DIXMUDE bridge-head, but here also the ever-rising flood soon prevented movement, and on the evening of the 1st these brave troops also had to yield to the forces of nature and withdraw behind the YSER. This operation was carried out in bright moonlight on the night of the 1st-2nd, and was unmolested by the enemy, for he lay in his position exhausted and heedless. Thus for the time being DIXMUDE remained in possession of the French.

The Army Commander had issued definite instructions on the evening of the 24th October to the XXIII, XXVI and XXVII Reserve Corps to the effect that they were to maintain and strengthen their positions, and take every opportunity of seizing important points on their immediate front. In the execution of this order the German troops experienced a good deal of heavy fighting during the subsequent days. The XXVII Reserve Corps succeeded in capturing REUTEL and holding it; [1] but in the meantime heavy hostile attacks were begun against the XXIII, XXVI and the extreme right wing of the XXVII Reserve Corps. The British, continually reinforced by the arrival of French units, endeavoured to break through, and used all their strength. Indeed, in many places the

---

[1] *The hamlet of Reutel had fallen into German hands on 24th October (cf. page 43, note), but the counter-attacks of the 2nd Division had re-established the line on the eastern border of Polygon Wood, and between 24th October and the morning of 29th October what changes there were on the eastern face of the Ypres salient had been in favour of the British. The 6th Infantry Brigade made considerable progress east of the Werwicq–Staden road in co-operation with the French IX Corps which pushed east and north-east from Zonnebeke. By the showing of this narrative the German forces in this area were decidedly superior in numbers to those engaged in the attacks.*

situation of these German volunteer corps became critical. Thanks to his good observation posts the enemy was able to keep our roads of advance and communications under artillery fire. As the roads were already broken up by the constant rain, the ammunition supply of our artillery, inferior in any case to our opponents', failed. Nevertheless, in spite of all difficulties our counter-attacks continued. The fighting was especially severe on the front of the XXVI and XXVII Reserve Corps on 25th, 26th and 27th October. In this sector the British and French made a succession of attacks in the direction POELKAP-PELLE, PASSCHENDAELE and east of ZONNEBEKE. The 37th *Landwehr* Brigade and the 2nd *Ersatz* Brigade, under the command of General von Meyer, had to be sent up into the fighting line, in addition to detachments of the Marine Division and of the 38th *Landwehr* Brigade. These *Landwehr* men, far from being weighed down by their years, gave effective support to the terribly thinned ranks of their younger friends, and the line was restored. In the heat of the fighting on the evening of the 26th General von Meyer was mortally wounded : may his memory be duly honoured.

An exceptionally heavy British and French attack was delivered on the 24th and 25th near ZONNEBEKE, against the inner flanks of the XXVI and XXVII Reserve Corps. The points of junction of formations are always the weakest parts of the defence, and when the General Staff Officer of the XXVII Reserve Corps asked for the support of the Corps on his right, he received the reply that no infantry could be spared ' for the enemy. . . .' And at that moment the telephone circuit failed. There was nothing to do but close the gap between the two Corps by an artillery barrage, and to trust to the skill of the troops and their leaders. The Saxon gunners of the 53rd Reserve Division shelled the advancing enemy as fast as they were able, and by this aid the infantry was finally enabled to come up and close the gap again. At the same time the enemy made a strong attack further to the south. The report came in that he had surrounded BECELAERE ; but before his supports could assist him, the bayonets of the 54th Reserve Division had driven back his assaulting troops.[1] The Corps was able to hold its old line from the cross-roads east of ZONNEBEKE through REUTEL to POEZELHOEK. Comparative quiet followed on the 28th and morning of the 29th, for both sides were very exhausted. On the 28th the 6th Bavarian Reserve Division arrived at DADIZEELE as Army Reserve.

The Army Cavalry of the Sixth Army, consisting of eight Cavalry Divisions and several *Jäger* battalions under General von der Marwitz, was in action on the left of the Fourth Army. It closed the gap between the latter and the infantry of the Sixth Army, which lay half-way between WARNETON and ARMENTIÈRES.

---

[1] *The above account presumably refers to the attack of the 18th French Division and 2nd British Division on 25th October, when a German battery was captured by the 1st Royal Berkshires and the French unit with which they were co-operating. Further to the British right, however, less progress was made, but the implication that the British reached Becelaere and were then thrust back by the 54th Reserve Division at the point of the bayonet is unfounded : the force engaged on this quarter only consisted of two battalions and the artillery support available was insufficient to allow the advance to be pressed home ; it was therefore abandoned after a small gain of ground had been made.*

The enemy could not be attacked here by any form of mounted action ; so far from this being possible, ground could be gained only by wearisome fighting on foot, to which the cavalrymen were unaccustomed. Nevertheless they carried out this task in brilliant fashion, and whilst the southern wing, in a bad position and scarcely entrenched at all, stubbornly held up the British who were streaming down from the high ground about WYTSCHAETE and MESSINES,[1] the 3rd, 7th and Bavarian Cavalry Divisions, with the 4th, 9th and 10th *Jäger* battalions and five battalions of the 11th *Landwehr* Brigade brought forward from Lille, advanced under General von Stetten to the assault of the line KRUISEIK–ZANDVOORDE and west of it. This direction was taken in order to be able to attack from the south against the rear of the enemy holding up the XXVII Reserve Corps. The 25th to 29th October were memorable and glorious days for this Cavalry Corps. Among other achievements, the 3rd Cavalry Division was able to capture KRUISEIK on the 26th after heavy street fighting.[2] In co-operation with the left wing of the XXVII Reserve

---

[1] *The British who were streaming down from the high ground about Wytschaete and Messines consisted of five brigades of cavalry (perhaps 4000) and one brigade of the newly arrived Lahore Division.*

[2] *There was very severe fighting south of the Menin road during the period 25th–28th October, particularly at Kruiseik, which formed the south-eastern angle of the east face of the salient. This position was obstinately defended by the 20th Infantry Brigade, 7th Division, which held on under heavy bombardments and repulsed many attacks, notably on the night of the 27th–28th October when over 200 of the 242nd Reserve Infantry Regiment (XXVII Reserve Corps) who had penetrated into Kruiseik were captured by a counter-attack of one company 2nd Scots Guards. The Germans renewed their attack in great force next day, and succeeded in dislodging the 20th Infantry Brigade from Kruiseik, but a new line was formed in rear, blunting the salient, and with the aid*

Corps, next to which the 16th Bavarian Reserve
Infantry Regiment of the 6th Bavarian Reserve
Division had been placed, taking a prominent part in
the fighting under Colonel List, General von Stetten,
on the 29th, carried forward the attack against GHELU-
VELT, the key of the enemy's position. More than
600 British prisoners and 5 machine-guns were taken
by our victorious cavalry.[1] Simultaneously on this
day, the troops of General von Stetten filled another
rôle. They were covering the concentration of new
German forces which was in the course of completion
behind their battle-front.

---

*of the 1st Division (in reserve since 24th October) the position was
successfully maintained.   Elsewhere the 7th Division, which was holding a line reaching back to Zandvoorde where the 3rd Cavalry Division
connected it up with the left of General Allenby's Cavalry Corps on the
Ypres–Comines canal, held its ground.*

[1] *This account does not tell the story of 29th October very intelligibly.
The British front had been readjusted, and was now held by the 2nd
Division on the left, from the junction with the French to west of Reutel,
thence to the 9th kilometre on the Ypres–Menin road by the 1st Division,
thence to Zandvoorde by the 7th Division with the 3rd Cavalry Division
on their right.   Under cover of a mist the Germans (apparently the
6th Bavarian Reserve Division) attacked in force against the junction
of the 1st and 7th Divisions, broke through at the 9th kilo cross-roads, and
rolled up the battalions to right and left after very severe fighting, in
which the 1st Grenadier Guards and 2nd Gordon Highlanders of the
7th Division distinguished themselves greatly by repeated counter-
attacks.   The resistance of the troops in the front line delayed the
Germans long enough to allow the reserves of the 1st Division to be put
in, and their counter-attacks recovered all but the most advanced trenches.
The Germans did not ever penetrate as far as Gheluvelt, and their final
gain of ground was inconsiderable.*

THE ATTEMPT TO BREAK THROUGH
SOUTH OF YPRES

THROUGHOUT the fighting of the Fourth Army during October, the Sixth Army under Crown Prince Rupert of Bavaria had remained on the offensive on the line ARRAS–LA BASSÉE–east of ARMENTIÈRES ;[1] but although fresh reinforcements had been sent up to that part of the front by the German General Staff, a break-through had not been possible. Both sides had gradually changed their objectives and now merely sought to prevent any movement of the opposing forces from that front to the decisive zone of operations between NIEUPORT and YPRES. Any weakness in the enemy's line, however, was utilised to gain new and improved positions from which another effort to break through might be made as soon as possible.

---

[1] *It is interesting to notice that this account treats the fighting on the La Bassée–Armentières front as quite distinct from the main battle for Ypres. During the period 20th-29th October the II and III Corps had a hard defensive battle to fight, the only assistance they received being on the arrival on 23rd October of the Jullundur Brigade and the divisional troops of the Lahore Division, which replaced General Conneau's French Cavalry at the junction between the two Corps. As the net result of this fighting the II and III Corps were forced back to a line running north by east from Givenchy, west of Neuve Chapelle, past Bois Grenier, south-east of Armentières to the Lys at Houplines, part of the 4th Division continuing the line on the left bank of the Lys to the junction with the Cavalry Corps just south of Messines. The German attacks on this front were strongly pressed, and the strain on the II and III Corps was very severe.*

Owing to the failure of the offensive south of NIEU-
PORT, a decision under the conditions existing there
could not be hoped for ; the German General Staff
therefore began considering a plan for concentrating
a strong new army of attack between the Fourth and
the Sixth Armies behind the position occupied by the
Army Cavalry, and for breaking through with it on
the front WERWICQ–WARNETON, south of YPRES.

On 27th October Lieut.-General von Falkenhayn
arrived at the Headquarters of the Sixth Army to
discuss this operation. The plan was arranged and
orders were issued accordingly. A new ' Army Group '
was to be affiliated to the Sixth Army, under the
command of General von Fabeck, commander of the
XIII Würtemburg Corps.[1] It would consist of the
II Bavarian and the XV Corps (now on its way up
from the south to join the Sixth Army), the 6th
Bavarian Reserve Division (still in reserve to the
Fourth Army), and the 26th Würtemburg Division
(of the Sixth Army, which was about to be relieved by
the 48th Reserve Division recently arrived from the
Fifth Army). In addition to these formations all
the available heavy artillery of the Sixth Army would
be brought up to assist, and if necessary the attacks
further south would be partially discontinued. The
offensive was to take place on the 30th October from
the general line WERWICQ–DEULEMONT in a north-
easterly direction. In the meantime the 3rd Division

---

[1] *In view of the reiterated statements about the superior numbers
of the Allies, it is worth pointing out that this new Army Group by itself
amounted to about two-thirds of the original strength of the British
forces engaged between La Bassée and Zonnebeke. For its Order of
Battle see at end of book.*

of the II Corps was also to be brought up by rail to LILLE. The orders of the German General Staff pointed out that the united co-operation of the Fourth and Sixth Armies was an essential condition for the success of the operation. Crown Prince Rupert of Bavaria therefore ordered the entire right wing and centre of the Sixth Army to continue their holding attacks, and Duke Albert of Würtemburg ordered a general attack of his Army for the 30th October.

How the flooding of the YSER on the front of the right wing of the Fourth Army brought the offensive of the III and XXII Reserve Corps to a standstill has already been described. From the 1st November the 4th *Ersatz* Division took over the protection of the line of the flooded area from the coast to TERVAETE, whilst the III Reserve Corps was moved southwards to the district ZARREN–STADEN in order to reinforce the XXIII or XXVI Reserve Corps, as the situation might require.[1] To the XXII Reserve Corps was allotted the task of holding the two French divisions stationed in the DIXMUDE bridge-head, which formed a constant threat to the German front. The Corps carried out this task admirably.

On the morning of the 30th October the XXIII, XXVI and XXVII Reserve Corps advanced to the attack as ordered. The first-named under General von Kleist succeeded in storming and holding the ruins of BIXSCHOOTE. After five hours' desperate

---

[1] *If the flooding of the country by the Belgians had barred the further advance of the Germans along the coast, it had equally covered the German extreme right against any chance of a counter-attack, and enabled them to divert the III Reserve Corps to the south ; the Belgians, however, were in no position to deflect any forces to the assistance of their Allies.*

fighting, the 211th and 216th Reserve Infantry Regiments entered the devastated village which had been occupied by two French infantry regiments. Its lowlying situation, and the hopelessness of finding cover among the battered houses, resulted in the victorious German regiments being exposed to a very heavy artillery fire to such an extent, that the casualties in the village were greater than during the assault. In consequence the commander decided to withdraw and take up a line along the northern edge of BIXSCHOOTE, leaving in the village itself only sufficient outposts to repulse hostile counter-attacks. The division on the left wing of the Corps also made progress and reached the main road BIXSCHOOTE–LANGEMARCK in places. The XXVI Reserve Corps attacked LANGEMARCK with its right wing, but was unable to take it. In spite of gallant efforts only a few hundred yards of ground were gained by the evening of the 31st, when these useless attacks were stopped by order. The centre and left wing of this Corps as well as the right wing of the XXVII Reserve Corps were held to their positions by superior hostile artillery fire, and also by mass attacks of the British and French during the 30th and 31st. The II and IX French Corps had just arrived, and in the presence of General Joffre an attempt to break through our line was to be made on this sector of the front.[1] The German defenders, however, held stoutly to their positions, and thus enabled the offensive of the Army Group of General

---

[1] *No mass attacks were made by the British on 30th and 31st October. It will be noticed that the French IX Corps is spoken of here as though it had been an additional reinforcement ; it had been in action on the Zonnebeke area since 24th October.*

von Fabeck to take place. In conjunction with this the centre and left wing of the XXVII Reserve Corps, under its new commander, General von Schubert, simultaneously advanced in the direction of GHELU-VELT.

During the night of the 27th-28th October the 26th Infantry Division was relieved in its battle-position west of LILLE by the 48th Reserve Division, and by the evening of the 29th the assembly of the Army Group Fabeck was completed without disturbance.

The heavy artillery placed at the disposal of the Army Group consisted of 8 batteries of mortars, 20 battalions of heavy field-howitzers, each of 3 batteries, and a 30·5 cm. coast defence mortar.[1] In addition to the troops already mentioned, the 1st Cavalry Corps, the four *Jäger* battalions of the Army Cavalry and the 11th *Landwehr* Brigade were put under the command of General von Fabeck. On the night of the 30th October this new army of attack relieved the two northern Cavalry Corps, and took over their outpost lines. On the following morning the offensive began.[2] The XV Corps under General von Deimling attacked south of the MENIN–YPRES road, with its left wing on

---

[1] *The heavy artillery at the disposal of the British Commander-in-Chief amounted at this time to two batteries of 6-inch howitzers, six of 60-pounders, and three of 4·7-inch guns, a total of forty-four guns and howitzers in all (each battery having four guns).*

[2] *At this time the Allied line from the Menin road south was held by the 7th Division, supported by about two infantry brigades of the I Corps, the line being carried on thence to Messines by part of the XVI French Corps and British Cavalry Divisions, and two battalions of the Lahore Division. Nearly all these units had been heavily engaged for a week or more, and were much under strength, but even at full war establishment would have been outnumbered by nearly two to one.*

ZANDVOORDE, the II Bavarian Corps was on its left, with
its left wing on WAMBEKE ; further south again was the
26th Infantry Division with its left wing on MESSINES.
In co-operation with these the 1st Cavalry Corps with
the 4th and Guard Cavalry Divisions, strengthened
by two battalions of the XIX Saxon Corps, which
was attacking to the left of it, was ordered to advance
on ST. YVES and PLOEGSTEERT Wood. The 6th
Bavarian Reserve Division moved to the line MENIN-
WERWICQ. The Army Cavalry which had been relieved was withdrawn to act as reserve to the Sixth
Army, one Cavalry Corps being placed behind the
right wing of the Army to be at hand to fill up a slight
gap which existed between the Fourth Army and the
Army Group Fabeck should it be necessary.

The enemy had intercalated part of the XVI French
Corps between the 7th Division of the IV British
Corps and the British Cavalry Corps, before the advance of von Fabeck's Army ; the II and IX French
Corps had also recently arrived [1] on the northern side of
the YPRES salient.*   Again, therefore, the enemy had
a numerical superiority [2] in what was the second and
severest part of the battle on the YSER.   The British

* See page 62.

[1] *See note, page 62.   The IX French Corps is mentioned for the third
time as a new arrival.*

[2] *It is difficult to see how this assertion can be supported on the statements previously given, even apart from the fact that the German units
were fresh and the British troops facing them reduced by previous heavy
losses.   The British claim to have held out against great odds is no more
than the bare truth.   The battalions of the 1st Division who had held
up the attack of the 46th Reserve Division north-west of Langemarck on
23rd October were still in the line when the Prussian Guard attacked
on 11th November—or rather a scanty remnant of them was :   in the
interval they had fought and held up a succession of attacks.*

in their reports have added together all the German
Corps which were brought up piecemeal for the fighting on the YSER and at YPRES, both at this period
and later on ; and they describe the situation so as
to give the impression that they had held up with
inferior numbers the simultaneous attacks of all these
Corps from the outset. They go further and use the
figures obtained in this way to turn their defeat into
a victory. They boast of having held out against
great odds, gladly forgetting that their original intention both before and during the battle had been to
overrun our positions and drive us back to the Rhine.

The character of the fighting which began with the
appearance of the new German Army Group on the
scene had almost the savagery of the Middle Ages in
it. The enemy turned every house, every wood and
every wall into a strong point, and each of them had
to be stormed by our men with heavy loss. Even
when the first line of these fortifications had been
taken they were confronted by a second one immediately behind it ; for the enemy showed great skill
in taking every advantage of the ground, unfavour-
able in any case to the attacker. To the east and
south-east of YPRES, even more developed than in
the north, there were thick hedges, wire fences and
broad dykes. Numerous woods also of all sizes with
dense undergrowth made the country almost impass-
able and most difficult for observation purposes. Our
movements were constantly being limited to the roads
which were swept by the enemy's machine-guns.
Owing to the preparatory artillery bombardments
the villages were mostly in ruins by the time the
infantry reached them, but the enemy fought desper-

E

ately for every heap of stones and every pile of bricks before abandoning them. In the few village streets that remained worthy of the name the fighting generally developed into isolated individual combats, and no description can do adequate justice to the bravery of the German troops on such occasions. Our men advanced to the attack as if they were back on the barrack square, and an Englishman writes : ' They advanced towards us singing patriotic songs and with their bands playing.' There was such enthusiasm that even the weakest were carried along by it, and made regardless of losses. The battle of YPRES in the autumn of 1914 will be a memorial to German heroism and self-sacrifice for all time, and will long remain a source of inspiration for the historian and the poet.

By the 29th Field-Marshal French had realised the importance of the attacks developing from the southeast against YPRES. They threatened his position along the high ground on the line GHELUVELT–PASSCHENDAELE and aimed directly at, and by the shortest way to, the town, the pivot on which all the Franco-British offensive plans rested. On this day, therefore, the British commander sent up the 7th Division into the line again, although it had only just been relieved owing to its heavy losses.[1]

Daybreak on the 30th October was dull and misty. Our heavy guns began the bombardment of the enemy's well-constructed lines at about 7.45 A.M., but observation was made very difficult by the weather condi-

---

[1] *The 7th Division had never left the line ; a few battalions only had been given a day's rest, but the division as a whole had not been relieved.*

tions, and could only be carried out from the foremost
infantry lines. The telephonic communication rendered necessary was frequently cut by the enemy's
shells ; but, in spite of this, our heavy batteries were
able to make such excellent practice that at the most
vital points of the enemy's position the spirit of the

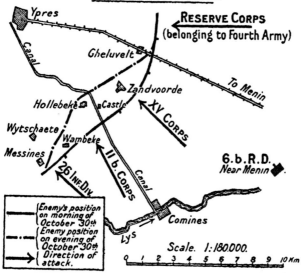

The ATTACK of the ARMY GROUP FABECK.
ON OCTOBER 30TH 1914.

defenders appeared to be completely broken. The
high ground about ZANDVOORDE offers a typical case.
Although only 130 feet high, it was a corner-stone of
the British defence and one of the main observation
posts for the artillery. At 9 A.M. our troops charged
the hostile position there, and by 11 A.M. ZANDVOORDE
itself was in the possession of the 30th Infantry Division ; the 4th, 10th and 1st Bavarian *Jäger* battalions
of the Army Cavalry took a great share in the success.

Soon afterwards the high ground north-east and immediately west of the village fell into German hands. Two whole British squadrons with their machine-guns lay, dead and wounded, completely annihilated in one meadow on the battlefield.[1] Further south the II Bavarian Corps had driven back British cavalry supported by part of the III British Corps. After a severe hand-to-hand encounter it took possession of the château, and finally also of the village of HOLLEBEKE. The left wing of the Corps pushed forward as far as the WAMBEKE stream, north of the village of the same name, but had here to put in all its reserves to hold its ground against strong hostile counter-attacks.[2]

On the left of the Bavarians the 26th Infantry Division was engaged in heavy fighting, the position confronting it being a particularly strong one. It lay along a prominent ridge from 180 to 250 feet high,* running north and south, eastwards of Mount KEMMEL, and gave the enemy an extensive view eastwards over our lines. The defence of this ridge was greatly facilitated by the villages of WYTSCHAETE and MESSINES on it. These had been turned into fortresses, and were connected by deep trenches protected by

---

* Messines ridge.

---

[1] *These squadrons belonged to the 1st and 2nd Life Guards, each of which regiments had a squadron cut off when Zandvoorde was stormed. None of the III British Corps were in this area, the extreme left of the Corps being about the river Douve, south of Messines.*

[2] *There was no strong counter-attack in the Wambeke area : the very thin line of the 2nd Cavalry Division (perhaps 3000 rifles on a front of two miles) was forced back to a position much nearer Wytschaete and St. Eloi, where it received reinforcements amounting to about a brigade of French infantry.*

broad wire entanglements.[1] Owing to observation
difficulties, and to the misty weather preventing the
airmen from giving assistance, our artillery was
unable from its positions in the valley to bring a
sufficiently heavy bombardment on the enemy's lines ;
and, though the Würtemburg troops attacked with
great gallantry, the enemy was too well prepared for
the assault. On the right wing the 122nd Fusilier
Regiment (Emperor Franz Joseph of Austria) took
the fortified village of WAMBEKE, and on the left wing
the 51st Infantry Brigade worked forward slowly
towards MESSINES. The ridge north-east of the last-
named village was stormed, but the assault on the
locality itself, which was to have been delivered at
7.10 in the evening, could not get on owing to heavy
enfilade fire from the south which held back the
attackers some hundred yards away from its edge.[2]
The Cavalry Corps [3] had gained ground at first, but,
in consequence of their weakness in artillery, they
had been unable to take ST. YVES or to make progress
against the strongly fortified wood south-west of it.
The same story describes the day's work of the XIX
Corps [4] fighting to the south of the cavalry.

---

[1] *The amount of work it had been possible to do there in preparing
the position for defence had been very much restricted by lack of time
and want of labour. ' Deep trenches protected by broad wire entanglements ' is a much exaggerated statement.*

[2] *An attack was made by the Germans on Messines about this time,
but was decisively repulsed.*

[3] *I and II Cavalry Corps.   See Order of Battle.*

[4] *The Germans at one time broke the line of the 19th Infantry Brigade
on the right of the III Corps near Bois Grenier, but were dislodged
by a counter-attack by the 2nd Argyll and Sutherland Highlanders and
1st Middlesex. In Ploegsteert Wood there was also heavy fighting, the
1st Hampshires distinguishing themselves in particular by a very
stubborn resistance.*

On the extreme right wing of the Army Group also the attack on the 30th October had not had the success expected. The combined efforts of the 54th Reserve Division and the right wing of the 30th Division had not been able to carry us into GHELUVELT.[1] General von Deimling and Major-General Wild von Hohenborn went forward themselves into the front line to encourage the men, but the enemy defended his positions desperately, and held on firmly to the main points of his line. Another artillery bombardment was therefore considered necessary.

From the enemy's point of view, however, the situation was anything but rosy on the evening of the 30th October. The entry of General von Deimling's troops into ZANDVOORDE endangered the southern side of the YPRES salient, and the capture of HOLLEBEKE brought the Germans within three miles of YPRES itself. YPRES was indeed in danger. Field-Marshal French had put Indian troops into the fighting line on the 30th, and he now brought all the available British and French reserves towards the line ZANDVOORDE–HOLLEBEKE in order to support the 7th British Division, which had been fought to a standstill.[2] During the night, therefore, the fighting never

---

[1] *Except at Zandvoorde the German attacks north of the Ypres–Comines canal were not successful, and their success at Zandvoorde was brought to a standstill by the arrival of two battalions of the 1st Division under Brigadier-General Bulfin, and three of the 2nd Division under Brigadier-General Lord Cavan, whose intervention enabled a new line to be formed north-west of Zandvoorde. To the east of Zandvoorde the 7th Division was forced to fall back nearer to Gheluvelt, but east of Gheluvelt itself the Germans made no progress.*

[2] *The arrival of the Meerut Division on 29th October allowed some of the most exhausted units of the II Corps to be relieved on the front east of Festubert, south-east of Richebourg St. Vaast, west of Neuve*

ceased: attacks and counter-attacks continued along the whole front, and under cover of darkness the indefatigable Würtemburg troops again tried to storm MESSINES.

On the 31st October the Germans had at first but few fresh troops to meet the enemy's reinforcements ; [1] so the 6th Bavarian Reserve Division was brought up in readiness north of the LYS behind the II Bavarian Corps. General von Fabeck had from the outset realised that the WYTSCHAETE–MESSINES ridge was of decisive importance, and that every effort must be made to take it ; on the 31st, therefore, the main pressure was to be exerted along the southern sector of attack of the II Bavarian Corps.

According to the enemy's accounts the 31st October 1914 was one of the most critical days at his headquarters. For us it was a day of great glory, and the British state unreservedly in their reports of the fighting, that the bravery of our men was beyond all praise. It is true that this last October day of the first war-year did not give us YPRES, but our semicircle around the town became so reduced that it was brought within range of our artillery from three sides, and there could be no more threats of a big hostile offensive based on the YPRES district. The fact that neither the enemy's commanders nor their troops gave way under the strong pressure we put on them, but continued to fight the battle round YPRES, though their situation was most perilous, gives us an opportunity to acknow-

---

Chapelle, but these battalions were not destined to enjoy a very long spell of rest.

[1] *The 'reinforcements' which the Allies had received on 29th-30th October were not even sufficient to redress the balance against them. (See note 2, page 70.)*

ledge that there were men of real worth opposed to us who did their duty thoroughly.

At dawn on Sunday the 31st October, in fine weather, a heavy artillery bombardment of the new hostile positions was begun on a front of ten and a half miles. The enemy's batteries were not long in replying; being so difficult to locate they had not suffered much in the previous fighting. Terrific artillery fire lasted throughout the morning, the British and French shells fell long distances behind our lines, blocking streets and bridges, and devastating the villages as far back as the Lys, so that any regular transport of supplies became impossible. At GHELUVELT, however, the important northern corner of the Army Group Fabeck, the enemy's hail of shells had but little result, because our capture of the high ground at ZANDVOORDE had made the work of observation very difficult.

After sufficient artillery preparation the British stronghold of GHELUVELT was to be attacked from south and east simultaneously. Colonel von Aldershausen, commanding the 105th Infantry Regiment, was to direct the attack from the east. Besides two battalions of his own regiment, there were placed under his command the 1st Battalion of the 143rd Infantry Regiment and a strong mixed detachment from the 54th Reserve Division, mainly belonging to the 245th Reserve Regiment and the 26th Reserve *Jäger* Battalion. The 99th Infantry Regiment was to make the attack from the south.[1] During the morning, in spite of the

---

[1] *The troops holding Gheluvelt consisted of two battalions of the 3rd Infantry Brigade, with portions of two of the 2nd Infantry Brigade, at most 2000 men. Against these the Germans by their own account put in about eight battalions.*

heaviest fighting, no success was achieved, and isolated attacks were repulsed by British counter-movements. At about 11 A.M. our converging attack was begun. The commanders of the 54th Reserve and 30th In-

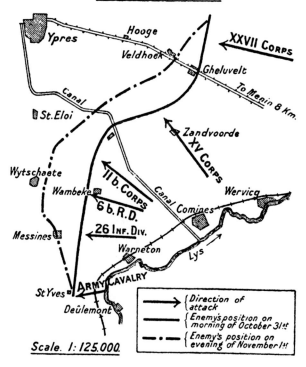

**The ATTACK of the ARMY GROUP FABECK.
ON OCTOBER 31ST 1914.**

fantry Divisions with their artillery leaders, as well as the general commanding the XV Corps, were again in the foremost lines, though the last, General von Deimling, was wounded almost at once by a shell-splinter. Towards midday the attack began to gain ground. His Majesty the Kaiser, who had arrived at the battle headquarters of the Sixth Army, watched the infantry working its way through the maze of the enemy's obstacles and entrenchments. It was well supported by artillery, some of the guns being moved forward with the front line. The British and French artillery fired as rapidly as they knew how,[1] and over every bush, hedge and fragment of wall floated a thin film of smoke, betraying a machine-gun rattling out bullets. But it was all of no avail: the attackers kept on advancing. More hostile strongholds were constantly being discovered; even all the points known to be of importance could not be given sufficient bombardments by our artillery, so that many attacks had to be delivered against fresh troops in good sheltered entrenchments untouched by our guns.[2] Many of our gallant men were killed, and the officers, who were the first to rise in the assault, were the special target of the enemy's sharpshooters, well trained in long colonial wars.[3] Once our troops entered an enemy's position, the resistance was only slight, and the German showed his superiority in single combat. It was only the enemy's counter-attacks, delivered with remarkable accuracy and rapidity, that regained some of his lost ground, but they did not, however, compromise the general success of the day.

---

[1] *It would not be gathered from this account that the British artillery had, as was the case, already been severely restricted as to ammunition expenditure.*

[2] *The statement that ' many attacks had to be delivered against fresh troops in good sheltered entrenchments ' is almost ludicrous in its travesty of the facts.*

[3] *It was not in ' long colonial wars ' but in careful training on the ranges that the majority of the defenders of Ypres had learnt that mastery of the rifle which was the mainstay of the success of the defence. Between the close of the South African War (1902) and the outbreak of war in 1914, scarcely any British troops had been on active service.*

The XXVII Reserve Corps pressed forward into the dense woods near REUTEL,[1] which were defended by a strong system of obstacles and by a quantity of machine-guns, hidden in some cases up in trees.[2]

While this was in progress the last assault on GHELU-VELT was taking place. The attacks from east and south both broke into the village, and by 3 P.M. the whole place with its château and park was in German possession.[3] Colonel von Hügel took his storming parties of the 54th Reserve Division northwards through and beyond the village, while Captain Reiner galloped his batteries close up to it. It was then, however, that fresh hostile reserves were launched against GHELU-VELT. The 16th Reserve Regiment of the 6th Bavarian Reserve Division was hurried up to meet them, its gallant commander, Colonel List, dying a hero's death

---

[1] *The position west of Reutel was maintained intact on 31st October, the right of the 2nd Division and left of the 1st Division holding on successfully even after the centre of the 1st Division had been pierced at Gheluvelt.*

[2] *The picture of the great profusion of machine-guns in the British possession is a little dimmed by the recollection that the war establishments allowed two machine-guns per infantry battalion, that by 31st October there had been no time to produce enough machine-guns to increase the establishment ; indeed, most battalions had already one or both their guns put out of action. The Germans clearly took for machine-gun fire the rapid fire which the infantry of the original Expeditionary Force could maintain.*

[3] *The capture of Gheluvelt was earlier than 3 p.m. by at least an hour, 1 or 1.30 p.m. seems more like the correct time. The ' château and park,' north of Gheluvelt, were held by the 1st South Wales Borderers, who maintained their ground, although their right was left in the air by the loss of the village, until the 2nd Worcesters came up and delivered their celebrated counter-attack past the right of the S.W.B. This apparently occurred about 2 p.m. The German account is, however, accurate in saying that Gheluvelt was not retaken ; what the Worcesters did was that they completely checked the German efforts to push forward ; the position their counter-attack reached enabled them to flank any advance west of Gheluvelt.*

during the movement. For a short time our own artillery fired into the backs of the Bavarian ranks : for the men were wearing caps and were thus mistaken for British troops. Nevertheless the enemy's counter-attack failed and GHELUVELT became and remained ours, and we captured besides 17 officers and 1000 men, and 3 guns.[1] The enemy prevented our further advance beyond GHELUVELT by a heavy fire from a new and strong position along the edge of the woods west of GHELUVELT. Here a new fortress had been made, which would have to be broken down by our artillery before it could be attacked. On the left wing of the XV Corps the German assaults also failed in front of some small woods which had been turned into strong points ; the 39th Infantry Division was able to advance only some 500 yards, though it took a number of prisoners.[2] The artillery of the XV Corps had an accidental success on this day which must have interfered with the enemy's staff work for some time. During the bombardment of HOOGE, a direct hit was made on a house in which the Staff of the 1st British Division were working : one general and several staff officers were killed.[3] After heavy fighting

---

[1] *The German claim to have captured three guns does not seem founded on fact : one gun of the 117th Field Battery was lost, but was subsequently retaken.*

[2] *The left of the XV Corps, which was in action against the detachments under Brigadier-Generals Bulfin and Lord Cavan, and the right of the 7th Division, in the woods later known as Shrewsbury Forest, was successfully held in check : it gained but a little ground, and at one point a most successful counter-attack drove the Germans back a long way, many casualties being inflicted and prisoners taken.*

[3] *The Staffs of both 1st and 2nd Divisions were there. Major-General Lomax, commanding the 1st Division, and Major-General Munro, commanding the 2nd Division, were wounded. Neither was killed, but the former died many months after of his wounds.*

at close quarters the II Bavarian Corps gained ground along the whole of its wide sector of attack on the 31st October. The right wing took possession of the edges of the woods west of HOLLEBEKE, whilst the left of the Corps advanced as far as OOSTTAVERNE. The 6th Bavarian Reserve Division had been brought into line immediately south of it, in order to make the attack on WYTSCHAETE.

We now come to the most vital point of the battle : who was to be the victor in the fight for the WYT-SCHAETE–MESSINES ridge ? The 6th Bavarian Reserve Division had worked forward by daylight towards WYTSCHAETE, regardless of the heavy artillery fire directed from the high ground on our troops moving up from the valley.[1] At nightfall the left wing of the II Bavarian Corps was still hanging back, unable to break the strong resistance opposed to it, but in spite of this the Bavarian Reserve Division dared to make its attack. The 17th Reserve Infantry Regiment was to enter WYTSCHAETE from the east and the 21st from the south. All the preparations had been carefully made. The men wore white arm-bands as a distinguishing mark when at close quarters with the enemy in the darkness. Water bottles were packed away in the haversacks ; rifles were unloaded and bayonets fixed. It was hoped to take the enemy by

---

[1] *During the course of 31st October French reinforcements of the XVI Corps had arrived and were taking over the left of the line held by the Cavalry Corps, relieving the 3rd and 5th Cavalry Brigades north-west of Hollebeke and south-east of St. Eloi. The French were, however, unable to make much ground by their counter-attacks, and further to the British right the 4th Cavalry Brigade was heavily pressed. It was here that the London Scottish were put in to recover trenches which had been lost east of the Messines–Wytschaete road.*

surprise, and not a light betrayed our arrival in the assembly positions. The hostile artillery fire slackened during the night, but frequent star-shells lighted up the darkness and showed that our opponents were keeping a careful watch. The clear moon must have helped them to see our movements. At 2 A.M. (1st Nov.) the Bavarians advanced from their assembly positions, taking little notice of the enemy's artillery which began to open on them. The general direction of the attack was given by the windmill of WYTSCHAETE, which was clearly outlined in the moonlight against the sky. The 17th Reserve Infantry Regiment under Colonel Hofmann rapidly reached the edge of the village and pushed through to the western exit. The surprise had succeeded, and numbers of the enemy who still held out in isolated ruins were either killed in a hand-to-hand fight, or taken prisoner.[1] Unfortunately, however, our own guns continued to bombard the village, as the news of the victory of the 17th Regiment was not communicated to them sufficiently quickly. At about 6 A.M. Colonel Hofmann there-

---

[1] *Accurate details of the fighting which went on through the night of 31st October-1st November round Wytschaete are extremely difficult to disentangle. It seems that the 4th Cavalry Brigade was forced out of the village somewhere between 2 and 3 a.m., that the advance of the Germans was then held up west of the village, counter-attacks by two battalions of the 3rd Division, which had just arrived from La Bassée-Neuve Chapelle area, assisting to check them. Subsequently these battalions (1st Northumberland Fusiliers and 1st Lincolnshires) were also forced back, but by this time more French reinforcements were coming up with some of the 5th Cavalry Brigade, and their counter-attacks, though not wholly successful, prevented further German progress. But the admission of this account that two whole German regiments (six battalions) were engaged in the attack is a fine testimony to the resistance made by the 2nd Cavalry Division and attached infantry at Wytschaete with odds of more than two to one against them.*

fore decided to withdraw his victorious troops temporarily to the eastern edge of WYTSCHAETE, and to reorganise there. It so happened that the 21st Reserve Regiment arrived on the southern side of the village at this moment, its advance having been delayed by a heavy enfilade fire from the south-west. When the men of the 21st Regiment in the first dim light of dawn saw the figures of men wearing caps running eastwards among the ruins, they immediately opened fire on them. Nevertheless, in spite of the losses incurred through this mistake, the 17th Regiment held its ground at the eastern edge of the village. The error was quickly remedied by singing patriotic songs and by flag-signals, and communication was regained with the neighbouring infantry and with the artillery. A strong counter-attack, however, was now made by six regiments of the XVI French Corps, which had arrived during the night, and the gallant 17th had slowly to withdraw again from the high ground.

The fighting around MESSINES on the 31st had been equally severe. On the 30th the 26th Infantry Division under Duke William of Urach had already got its patrols up to the edge of the village, but before any assault could be made an artillery preparation was required, especially against the northern sector. On the morning of the 31st October our howitzers and trench-mortars bombarded the enemy in his trenches, and by 10.30 A.M. the moment had arrived for the Würtemburg troops to advance.

The 122nd Fusilier Regiment was to attack the ridge north of MESSINES, along which runs the road to WYTSCHAETE, whilst the 125th Infantry Regiment was to advance against MESSINES itself, and the 119th

Grenadier Regiment against the enemy's trenches immediately south of it. The hostile position was so strong that a force greatly inferior in strength would be able to hold it against an attack coming up from the valley. Bare sloping ground lay in front of it, and only a few hedges limited the field of view, so that every advance and assembly position for miles round could be seen. A strong British garrison held MESSINES: the trenches had been well made, and were covered by a continuous and broad system of obstacles.[1]

The way in which the Swabian troops [2] broke down the enemy's resistance was indeed a masterpiece. Neither the enemy's artillery fire, which imperilled the advance of the reserves, nor the British machine-guns, a large number of which enfiladed the attack from the south, could restrain the dash of the Würtemburg troops. At 11 A.M. the 125th Stuttgart Infantry Regiment had got possession of the north-east corner of MESSINES. The road entering the village from GAPAARD was blocked by a barricade; and after storming it, another one, a hundred yards further inside the village, closed the way. The streets could not be used for our advance, being choked with debris, and under heavy rifle and machine-gun fire, so the attackers had to make their way through or over the walls.

---

[1] *The forces available for the defence of Messines were the 1st Cavalry Division, much reduced by the previous fighting, assisted by portions of the 57th Rifles (Lahore Division) and two battalions of the 5th Division (the 2nd King's Own Scottish Borderers, 2nd King's Own Yorkshire L.I., both recently relieved from the trenches near Neuve Chapelle and much below strength). The twelve battalions of the 26th (Würtemburg) Division were thus in overwhelming superiority. The only artillery available to assist the defence were the 13-pounders of the R.H.A. batteries attached to the Cavalry Corps.*

[2] *i.e. Würtemburg.*

There are a number of large, well-built houses in
MESSINES, which the enemy had turned into a succession of strongholds, but they were rapidly blown up
by our sappers. The convent looked especially impregnable with its walls a yard thick, and strong

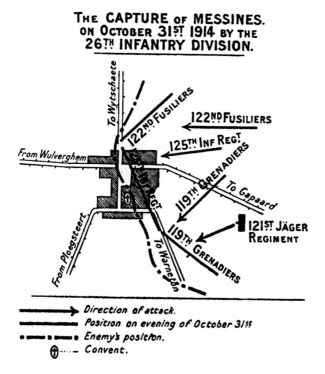

THE CAPTURE OF MESSINES.
ON OCTOBER 31ST 1914 BY THE
26TH INFANTRY DIVISION.

Direction of attack.
Position on evening of October 31st
Enemy's position.
Convent.

towers from which machine-guns and rifles fired fran-
tically. Captain Heinrich's Würtemburg battery of
the 65th Field Artillery Regiment was therefore brought
up, the men dragging the guns through the streets, as
horses could·not move along them, and the infantry
carrying up the ammunition. The convent was soon
in flames, burying its stubborn defenders under its
ruins. Lieutenant Mösner of the 125th Infantry

Regiment, following a narrow footpath through gardens and backyards, was the first to make an entry into the market-square. With a few stout-hearted followers he occupied a large building there which he defended without any support till the evening against great odds. Not until nightfall were others of his regiment able to reach him, and secure the position he had held so courageously. This day of street fighting had cost very dear, and our casualty list was a large one. A part of the 122nd Fusilier Regiment fighting north of MESSINES had also had to be directed on to the village, and by the evening a continuous line had been successfully formed through the centre of it. Isolated fighting continued throughout the night, and in order to keep up communication amidst the ruins and recognise one another in the dark, the Würtemburg troops sang folk-songs. The chorus of voices mixed with the rattle of machine-guns, the roar of artillery in the streets, and the crackle of the burning and falling houses, all combined to make a magnificent and unsurpassed piece of battle-music.

North of the village the left wing of the 122nd Infantry Regiment established itself on the MESSINES–WYTSCHAETE road : but its right wing was unable to capture the high ground, as WYTSCHAETE itself was still in British hands. The 119th Grenadiers suffered severely : the progress of the other regiment of their brigade, the 125th Infantry Regiment, had roused their ambition, but a heavy enfilade fire swept their ranks from the south where the Cavalry Corps were still unable to advance. They were compelled by heavy losses to be content with the task of securing the left flank of their division.

On the evening of the 31st the gallant attackers were rewarded for their deeds of immortal fame by a message of warm praise from the Emperor.

The final objective, however, had not yet been attained, although in the south the high ground had been reached and artillery observers sent forward there, so that the enemy's positions could be accurately ranged on right up to Mount KEMMEL. The main pressure of the attack would therefore have to be continued here, on the left wing of the Army Group Fabeck.

During the 1st November the 3rd Infantry Division arrived in the area COMINES–WARNETON, north of the LYS, as reserve to the Army Group.

On the morning of the 1st November a thick mist lay over the country, so that the infantry got a few hours' rest before the continuous shelling of the enemy's artillery began. As soon as the mist cleared, the battle broke out anew, on a twelve-mile front. In the north the Saxon and Würtemburg divisions of the XXVII Reserve Corps further extended their successes of the previous days. The line was advanced up to the château of POEZELHOEK, which was taken from the 1st British Division after a heavy fight.[1]

The divisions of Deimling's XV Corps attacked with the right wing on the GHELUVELT–YPRES main road and the left on KLEIN ZILLEBEKE. They advanced

---

[1] *This is not accurate. Poezelhoek Château had to be evacuated during the night of 31st October–1st November, owing to the withdrawal of the line made necessary by the loss of Gheluvelt; but the Germans did not molest the retirement to the new position, and such attempts as they made in the course of 1st November to press on westward beyond Gheluvelt were unsuccessful. The British accounts do not give the impression that the German attacks on this day were very heavily pressed in this quarter; at any rate they failed to make any ground.*

but slowly, fighting hard the whole day. The small, dense woods, defended with the utmost tenacity, again made progress very difficult. The 30th Division managed to reach the eastern edge of the HEREN-THAGE Wood, where the 3rd British Cavalry Division, supported by infantry, was in position. The wood north of ZANDVOORDE gave exceptional trouble, but it was finally outflanked on both sides, and its defenders taken prisoner.[1]

The II Bavarian Corps advanced to the attack on both sides of the COMINES–YPRES canal, and drove the enemy back as far as the sharp bend in it. The left wing captured the small wood west of OOSTTA-VERNE which was defended by Indian and British troops. The treacherous methods of the Indians greatly exasperated our men : crouching in the hedges, and with machine-guns concealed up trees, the defeated Asiatics allowed our troops to pass them, and then got up and stabbed them in the back with their knives.[2] The 6th Bavarian Reserve Division had withdrawn, on

---

[1] *The hardest fighting of 1st November in the Ypres salient was in the area north-west of Zandvoorde where the detachments under Brigadier-Generals Bulfin and Lord Cavan were sharply engaged, as were also the remnants of the 7th Division, now holding a position south-east and south of the Herenthage Wood. A feature of this day's fighting was a counter-attack by the 26th Field Company R.E., acting as infantry in default of any infantry reserves, which checked the efforts of the Germans to advance north of Groenenburg Farm (north-west of Zandvoorde).*

[2] *The Indian units hitherto employed under the Cavalry Corps (57th Rifles and 129th Baluchis) had already been withdrawn to Kemmel, and were not in action near Oosttaverne on 1st November. This account of the 'treacherous methods of the Indians' smacks of the conventional ; it is what was attributed to the Ghurkhas in some sections of the German Press, and seems inserted rather to excite odium against the British for calling in Asiatics to oppose the disciples of 'Kultur.'*

the morning of the 1st November, to its positions of
the previous evening, and at midday began its attack
once more. Confidence and enthusiasm served to
obliterate the bad memories of the past night, and the
dense lines now rose simultaneously from their positions as if on parade. Very many of their dead or
wounded still lay at the foot of the heights, but the
gallant division stormed the slopes again, and by
4 P.M. had reached the eastern edge of WYTSCHAETE.
It was not possible to push up reserves owing to heavy
artillery fire, and at this moment the enemy counter-
attacked with two fresh divisions.[1] The Bavarians,
who had become disorganised during the assault, were
forced to evacuate the village again under cover of
darkness, after having actually entered it at about
5 P.M. They had suffered very heavily during the
attack, being fired at from flank and rear, for the right
wing of the 26th Infantry Division was unable to
take all the high ground north-west of MESSINES until
the evening of the 1st November. Fierce street fighting had gone on in MESSINES throughout the day, till
finally the Würtemburg troops gained the upper hand
and cleared the enemy out of the village to its western
edge. The British were driven back down the western
slope of the ridge, and had to entrench themselves in
the valley, losing heavily in the operation. As soon
as its right wing reached the MESSINES–WYTSCHAETE
road that evening the 26th Infantry Division held
almost the whole of the famous ridge, and the pre-
liminary condition for the capture of WYTSCHAETE

---

[1] *French Divisions. By the afternoon of 1st November the French
had taken over the defence of Wytschaete. The 2nd Cavalry Division
assembled on a line east of Kemmel and Wulverghem.*

was obtained. The 6th Bavarian Reserve Division, however, was not able to carry out a third assault without assistance, and General von Fabeck during the night of the 1st-2nd therefore advanced the 3rd Prussian Division from its assembly area WAMBEKE–GARDE DIEU into the fighting line, in order to carry forward the attack through and beyond WYTSCHAETE towards KEMMEL.

After a comparatively quiet night the battle opened again on the morning of the 2nd November along the whole front of the Army Group Fabeck. His indefatigable troops, some of whom had already endured twelve days of the heaviest fighting that had taken place in the campaign, attacked their strongly entrenched opponent once more. The enemy was at least as strong as they were in fighting units on the battle-front, and besides was able to bring up reinforcements of newly arrived British and French troops.[1]

On the eastern side of the YPRES salient General von Deimling attacked on a front of nearly four miles. His Corps, which had won its laurels in Alsace, in Lorraine and in Northern France, again, in spite of heavy casualties, continued its advance of the previous days. The 30th Division entered VELDHOEK and established itself firmly in the north-eastern corner of the HEREN-THAGE Wood.[2] The attack had been facilitated by

---

[1] *These ' reinforcements of newly arrived British troops ' are imaginary.*

[2] *The Germans, attacking along the Menin road, succeeded in breaking our line at this point and captured two guns which had been pushed up into the front trenches. However, the 1st Scots Guards, though taken in flank, held on north of the road till a counter-attack by the 1st Black Watch re-established the line, while south of the road a counter-attack*

a simultaneous advance of the XXVII Reserve Corps,
which had pressed forward some hundred yards north
of VELDHOEK.   Von Deimling's left wing had advanced
in the direction of KLEIN ZILLEBEKE, but was held up
by the difficult wooded country east of ZWARTELEEN.
It had to wait here for assistance from the neighbouring
troops on its left.

The II Bavarian Corps had been held up early on
the morning of the 2nd November by strong hostile
counter-attacks in the sector west of HOLLEBEKE.
They were all, however, repulsed and the Corps was
even able to make a slight advance on the right wing
during the day.

WYTSCHAETE was again the centre of the heaviest
fighting on this day.[1]   The Bavarian Reserve Division was, at its own request, to attack the village ; the
enemy's position immediately south of it was allotted
as objective to the 3rd Division.   The 42nd Infantry
Regiment and an *Abtheilung* (3 batteries) of the
17th Field Artillery Regiment remained in Army
Reserve.   At 7 A.M. a fierce artillery duel began, and
the enemy, quickly realising the danger threatening
him, hurried up strong reserves to WYTSCHAETE.
Kiefhaber's brigade of the 6th Bavarian Reserve Division rose to the assault.   Under a hail of shrapnel

---

*by the remnants of the 2nd and 3rd Brigade cleared the Herenthage
Wood completely, but did not regain the front trenches a little eastward.
Further to the right Lord Cavan's detachment (Brigadier-General
Bulfin had been wounded on 1st November, and his battalions had come
under Lord Cavan's orders) and the remnants of the 1st Grenadiers
and 2nd Border Regiment (7th Division) held their own successfully
and inflicted very heavy losses on the Germans, i.e. Deimling's left
wing.*

[1] *The credit for the gallant defence of Wytschaete on this day belongs
solely to the French ; no British troops were in action there.*

the youngsters stormed the eastern and southern slopes of the WYTSCHAETE ridge for the third time, though with considerable loss, the enemy's machine-guns causing great havoc in their ranks. As soon as the foremost of them had reached the windmill the enemy launched a counter-attack ; but this time the Bavarians were not content with simply holding their ground ; their supports were brought up at the critical moment and pressed forward into the village. Furious street fighting now ensued, and the Bavarians having to deal with every house became greatly disorganised. Taking advantage of this the British and French commanders sent forward fresh masses into the line, trying to turn the balance in their favour at this important point by employing every available man. It was 3.10 P.M. when a cry for help reached the Pomeranian (3rd) Division from their Bavarian neighbours, and it was not uttered in vain. Shortly before, the Stettin Grenadier Regiment had captured the long-coveted high ground south-west of WYTSCHAETE, the struggle for a large farmhouse on it having been especially severe. Without possession of this the south flank of the village could not be held. Count Gneisenau's Colberg Grenadiers were then sent forward to support the Bavarians, and the enemy was unable to hold out in WYTSCHAETE against the rifle-butts and bayonets of the united Pomeranians and Bavarians. Soon after 5 P.M. the village, as far as its western edge, was in German hands, although the fighting continued till well into the night among the ruins with detachments of the enemy who would not surrender.

By the capture of WYTSCHAETE a fine commanding position had been obtained, but the village itself, once so pleasant to the view, was now terrible to look upon. The church was in flames, and the windmill flared like a beacon in the darkness. Friend and foe lay wounded side by side among the smouldering ruins. The enemy was fully aware of the importance of WYTSCHAETE, but he had been so weakened that he was unable to recover for another big counter-attack. He therefore contented himself with small and fruitless efforts, only one of which succeeded in temporarily entering the village during the 3rd. Nevertheless for the next few days it lay under the constant fire of heavy artillery, though our heroic observers did not allow this to interfere with their work.

Many of the inhabitants still remained in WYTSCHAETE, as in MESSINES, and it was pathetic to see how they clung to their devastated patches of ground, regardless of danger. In spite of many offers from the Germans, these Belgian inhabitants remained with their last scrap of property, preferring to die by the shell that destroyed their homes.

A small wood north-west of WYTSCHAETE, called the Park, was still a dangerous point. This dense copse was surrounded by a system of trenches and several rows of obstacles. With the help of skilfully sited flanking arrangements and shell-proof shelters, it had been turned into an almost impregnable stronghold, and cost us many days of heavy fighting before it was finally taken.

The 26th Infantry Division, after its capture of MESSINES, immediately put the high ground into a state of defence. Its left brigade, the 51st, which was in position there, was relieved on the 2nd November by the 11th *Landwehr* Brigade, and sent back to the

Army Reserve. The 52nd Brigade, on the right wing of the division, in co-operation with the 3rd Infantry Division, advanced across the STEENBEEK stream. However, no progress of importance could be made there, as every movement could be immediately brought under most effective artillery fire from the commanding positions on Mount KEMMEL.[1]

On the 3rd November the formation of a ' Group Urach ' was ordered, consisting of the 3rd and 26th Infantry Divisions, to continue the attack against the high ground east of KEMMEL ; but in the following days it was unable to make any essential alteration in the general situation in this sector.

A part of the Army Cavalry was still in action south of, and co-operating with, the 26th Infantry Division, in spite of the small force of artillery and engineers included in it. On the 2nd November it made a surprise attack on foot against the farm KLEIN DOUVE with complete success.[2] On the 4th November the I Cavalry Corps was relieved by the II, consisting of the 3rd and 7th Cavalry Divisions.

In the early days of November the conduct of the

---

[1] *After the capture of Messines and Wytschaete the severity of the fighting in this quarter died down rapidly.   The French made some attempts to recover Wytschaete, while the Germans managed to capture Hill 75 (Spanbroekmolen), but could advance no further, and the British Cavalry Corps established itself firmly in trenches north-east of Wulverghem.   Supported by the artillery of the 5th Division, it maintained itself on this line till relieved by the infantry of the 5th Division about the middle of November.*

[2] *The chaplain of the Guard Cavalry Division, ' Hofprediger ' Dr. Vogel, in his book ' 3000 Kilometer mit der Garde-Kavallerie ' (p. 212), says the attack was made and failed, but ' next day the English abandoned the farm : this may have been due either to the power of our 8 - inch howitzers, or to the moral effect of the attack of the Guard Dragoons.'*

enemy's operations against the Army Group Fabeck underwent a very noticeable change. The German attacks had destroyed any prospect of success for the big offensive movement which had been planned. The British troops, especially the I and IV Corps,[1] were so played out that they had to be relieved by parts of the French Army. The enemy's commanders, however, realised that even these fresh troops would be unable to make much headway against our men, and they therefore decided to remain on the defensive and to create a deep zone of trench-systems. The heavy fighting had made havoc of their front trenches, or at least had badly damaged them. The civil population and all other available labour, therefore, were now called upon to dig successive lines of rearward positions for a long way westwards.[2] These preparations were soon discovered by our airmen.

During the early days of November the commander of the Sixth Army came to the conclusion that the offensive of the Army Group Fabeck could lead to no

---

[1] *What other British troops were present in the Ypres salient except the I and IV Corps this narrative does not pause to state, for the simple reason that there were none.   The I Corps was not relieved, though some French battalions were put into the line near Veldhoek ; but in the course of 5th November the remnant of the infantry of the 7th Division was relieved by the two composite brigades from the II Corps composed of battalions which had had three weeks' fighting near La Bassée and had then to be thrust in after only two or three days' rest to hold some of the most difficult parts of the line south-east of Ypres.   The 7th Infantry Division when relieved amounted to less than a third of their original strength, without taking into account the drafts that had joined since they landed, which amounted to 2000 or more.   Most of the battalions of the 1st Division were in scarcely better case.*

[2] *These ' successive lines of rearward positions ' did not exist except on paper during the period to be included in the ' Battle of Ypres,' i.e. to 17th November.*

decisive results.   The forces available were still too
weak to break through the enemy's strongly entrenched
positions, particularly as he was continually bringing
up fresh reinforcements to the battle-front.

If the attempt to break through south of YPRES was
not to be entirely abandoned, and a purely defensive
war on the Western Front thereby avoided, more
troops would have to be brought up for the YPRES
battle from other sectors of the front.   As a beginning
the 2nd and the Bavarian Cavalry Divisions were
affiliated to the Army Group Fabeck, the Bavarian
Cavalry Division being allotted to the XV Corps and
the 2nd Cavalry Division to the II Bavarian Corps.
The German General Staff also placed the II Corps
and the 4th Infantry Division at the disposal of General
von Fabeck, and they began to detrain at LILLE on
the 5th November.   On the 3rd Crown Prince Rupert
of Bavaria ordered the XXIV Reserve Corps and the
25th Reserve Division to be taken fron the Sixth
Army, west of LILLE ; and this was followed by an
order on the 4th to withdraw all the troops of the
Guard Corps available from their positions, and for
their sector of the front to be taken over by the IV
Corps at ARRAS.   Accordingly a composite Division
of the Guard Corps, consisting of the 1st and 4th
Guard Infantry Brigades, under Lieutenant-General
von Winckler, marched for ROUBAIX, which was reached
on the 7th.   More heavy artillery was also handed
over to the Army Group Fabeck, and, in addition, all
the artillery ammunition allotted to the Sixth Army.
The intention of the German General Staff, communicated to the commander of the Sixth Army on
the 4th November, was : to push the attack to the

immediate north (of the elbow) of the COMINES–YPRES
canal, and to put in all available forces to break
through there. In the meantime, however, General
von Fabeck, in accordance with instructions previously
issued by the commander of the Sixth Army, had
placed the XXIV Reserve Corps and the 25th Reserve
Division on the left wing of the II Bavarian Corps,
and had there formed a Group Gerok, to which the
6th Bavarian Reserve Division was added. Thus for
the offensive north of the COMINES–YPRES canal there
were left the II Corps and Guard Corps (the 4th Division and the mixed Division of von Winckler), besides
the XV Corps which was already in position there.
The fighting continued along the front of the Army
Group until the 10th, when these troops were ready
to attack. No time was to be given the enemy to
recover, or to strengthen his positions.

The XV Corps, which in the meantime had extended
its left wing to the COMINES–YPRES canal, won ground
daily, especially on the 6th November, when the 39th
Division delivered a heavy attack near KLEIN ZILLE-
BEKE and drove the recently arrived French troops
from their position, capturing four hundred prisoners in
the farm buildings. The troops, advancing with their
bands playing, also stormed parts of ZWARTELEEN, a
village widely scattered among the woods and meadows.
The artillery fired at point - blank range, as the
November mist made observation impossible at any
distance. French counter - attacks and an attack
by British cavalry, which attempted to make good
the retirement of the French, were repulsed. Their
casualties were heavy, the 1st and 2nd British Life
Guards being decimated. The enemy's counter-attacks

on the 7th and 8th November, in which the much weakened 7th British Division, as well as the Zouaves, took part, had also no success. On the 8th November the 148th Infantry Regiment captured the fortified position along the western edge of VELDHOEK ; with a strong counter-attack the French made a bid to recover the lost ground. Lieutenant-Colonel Linker, the gallant regimental commander, hastily gathered together all the supports within reach, including *Landwehr* men of the 54th Reserve Division, and led them forward to meet the advancing enemy ; he himself was mortally wounded at the head of his victorious followers. The French hurriedly retired, suffering considerable loss.[1]

The II Bavarian Corps was kept busily employed by the hostile counter-attacks near the canal ; the enemy offered very stubborn resistance in order to keep possession of the high ground from which YPRES can be seen. The Bavarians, however, not only maintained their positions, but, by an irresistible attack on the 9th and 10th November, took the high ground

---

[1] *During the period 2nd-11th November the most serious fighting on the British front was between 6th and 8th November. On the 6th the Germans attacked near Zwarteleen and gained ground, some of which was recovered by a fine counter - attack delivered by the 7th Cavalry Brigade (cf. page 93, line 30), while further counter-attacks by the 22nd Infantry Brigade, brought back just as it had been drawn out for a rest, and by portions of the 1st Division further improved the line next day. On that day (7th November) a sharp attack on the 3rd Division, which had now taken over the line south of the Menin road, gained a little ground east of the Herenthage Wood. This part of the line was again attacked in force on 8th November, and the line was broken near Veldhoek, but was restored after some sharp fighting and several counter-attacks. Further north again, in Polygon Wood and to the east of it, the 2nd Division, though repeatedly attacked, more than held its own. In the fighting near Veldhoek a prominent part was taken by two battalions of Zouaves who had filled a gap in the line of the 1st Division.*

on which ST. ELOI is situated.[1]   To the 5th Bavarian
Infantry Brigade is due all the credit for this fine feat.
The enemy remained for a long time in the houses of
ST. ELOI, but the high ground was of primary, perhaps
even decisive, importance ; for it gave us a bird's-eye
view of the country east of YPRES, where the mass of
the British field artillery was in position.

The fighting further south which the troops of the
Group Gerok had in and north of WYTSCHAETE was
equally heavy.   The northern edge formed the divid-
ing line between the Groups Gerok and Urach.   The
enemy kept the village under heavy fire in order to
hinder the work of our observers, the mere sight of a
man anywhere being sufficient to draw his artillery
fire.   Our stereo-telescopes were therefore used through
loopholes in the ruins or at the chimney openings,
and the observers were often far safer on such lofty
perches than our reserves in the cellars of the battered
village.   Only slow progress could be made in the
woods lying to the north-west.

The Group Urach also was unable to make much
headway.   On its right wing, the 3rd Infantry Division struggled hard to get possession of the Park
north-west of WYTSCHAETE.   After a whole day's
fighting the 34th Fusilier Regiment forced its way
into the hospice, a fine old convent at the northern
entrance to the village ; from its roof the enemy had
been able to get a splendid view of our positions in
the valley south of WYTSCHAETE.   In spite of a most

---

[1] *St. Eloi is hardly situated ' on high ground,' as it is on the down
slope where the Warneton–Ypres road descends into the low ground
after crossing the north-easterly continuation of the Messines–Wytschaete ridge.*

thorough bombardment our attack was very costly, and although the Park was enveloped on two sides, it was found impossible to enter it. From this patch of wood heavy enfilade fire swept the positions of the 6th Bavarian Division to the north, and the trenches of the 3rd Prussian Division to the south. It was surrounded by a wall and moat as well as by wire entanglements, the impenetrable undergrowth being entangled with a maze of wire. Frenchmen with machine-guns were roped to the trunks of some of the trees, and they were found dead hanging from the shell-torn stumps when the Park of WYTSCHAETE was finally stormed on the 13th November by the 21st Reserve Infantry Regiment of the 6th Bavarian Division, with the 2nd Grenadiers and 34th Fusiliers of the 3rd Prussian Division. There is a legend connected with WYTSCHAETE Park, and the scene was worthy of it.[1]

The 26th Infantry Division during these days had advanced its lines to the western slopes of the WYTSCHAETE–MESSINES ridge, and in places across the valley, by sapping. This operation cost many casualties, as the British on Mount KEMMEL were able to watch every movement in our trenches, and could immediately bring them under the fire of field or heavy artillery, or even of long-range naval guns, and they were by no means sparing with their ammunition. Fortunately our losses were for the most part only in the front lines, but our shortage of ammunition compelled us to husband it.[2] Owing to the conformation

---

[1] *The allusion is not understood.*

[2] *The heavy artillery at Sir John French's disposal at this period was still extremely limited, and its effectiveness was greatly hampered*

of the ground and to the weather preventing any air-reconnaissances, we were unable to range accurately on the enemy's artillery, and the most we could do was to disturb their means of fire-direction. Their observation posts on Mount KEMMEL were soon discovered, and the fight now began against the observers there as well as against those posted in the towers of YPRES. So the blame must not be laid on us for the gradual destruction of those magnificent buildings of YPRES, which gave such a fine view of the whole countryside.

Further to the south no noteworthy progress was made either by the Cavalry Corps, or on the front of the Sixth Army.

Such then was the general situation when, on the 10th November, the new forces lay ready to take the offensive in their positions north of the COMINES–YPRES canal. Before going further, however, the operations of the Fourth Army from the last days of October must for a moment be touched on.

---

by the lack of ammunition, stringent restrictions having to be placed on the ammunition expenditure of guns of all calibres. Fortunately for the Allies a similar handicap was beginning to make itself felt among the Germans ; even their preparations had been hardly equal to the vast ammunition expenditure which had been incurred.

THE OPERATIONS OF THE FOURTH ARMY FROM THE END OF OCTOBER TO THE 9TH NOVEMBER 1914

WHILST the northern wing of the Sixth Army under General von Fabeck was engaged in the heavy fighting just described, the Fourth Army of Duke Albert of Würtemburg had been doing its utmost, by means of constant attacks, to prevent the enemy from withdrawing any troops from his front to support his endangered positions near YPRES. By 11 A.M. on the 3rd November the reorganisation of the German forces rendered necessary by the inundation of the front between the coast and DIXMUDE had been sufficiently completed to enable an offensive to be delivered on this day, on the line DIXMUDE–GHELUVELT. The right flank, from DIXMUDE to the coast, was secured by the 38th *Landwehr* Brigade, 4th *Ersatz* Division, and part of the 43rd Reserve Division, all under the orders of the general officer commanding the XXII Reserve Corps. The dispositions of the attacking troops were as follows : the XXIII Reserve Corps in the sector NOORDSCHOOTE–BIXSCHOOTE ; the III Reserve Corps, including the 44th Reserve Division, on both sides of LANGEMARCK, facing the front HET SAS–ST. JULIEN (this was the most important group in the offensive) ; the XXVI and XXVII Reserve

Corps were to the south again, with the left flank resting on the GHELUVELT–YPRES main road.[1]

By the evening of the 5th the XXIII Reserve Corps had been able to gain ground at and north of BIX-SCHOOTE, while the 5th Reserve Division advancing from the north had forced its way close up to the western edge of LANGEMARCK. But all our efforts to capture this place by attacks from north and east, in spite of reinforcements being brought up, failed. It became evident that the enemy's skilfully placed and more numerous artillery, combined with his well-wired infantry positions in a country so favourable for defence, were more than a match for our guns, especially at a time when ammunition was scarce, and the misty weather prevented observation from aeroplanes. A continuation of the offensive here would only have meant a useless sacrifice of life. It was therefore decided with deep regret to resort to the long and wearisome task of sapping in order to hold the enemy. The situation of the Fourth Army indeed was no enviable one. Here in the plains of Flanders, operations were effected by the November weather and heavy rains, far more than in the country east and south of YPRES. The troops had to endure great hardships; their trenches rapidly filled with water, and were necessarily so shallow as to give insufficient protection against artillery fire. In several places they had to be evacuated altogether, and the men lay out in the open with only a hastily constructed wire entanglement in front to secure them

---

[1] *The portion of the Ypres salient attacked by the XXIII Corps was defended by French troops alone ; there were no British north of the Broodseinde cross-roads.*

against surprise attacks. Sapping too proved most difficult in this water-logged district. Frequently it could only be carried on by piling up sand-bag parapets, and these being easily seen by the enemy were promptly shelled. Thus the attack made slow progress. Regular reliefs for the troops in the front line were out of the question, for the units available at that time were too weak ; and in any case, the men found relief time a very dangerous moment, as the enemy was able to observe every movement, especially where he still held good observation points, as at BIXSCHOOTE and LANGEMARCK.

A very extensive system of espionage served to complete his knowledge of our intentions. Individual soldiers were left behind in civilian clothing, with concealed telephonic communication ; they kept hidden during the daytime in attics and cellars, and reported our movements and dispositions quickly and accurately to their headquarters.[1] A great deal of information was also given away by the Belgian population, who crossed the German lines by secret bypaths, or sent news across by carrier-pigeons, or by lights and signals. Although the punishment meted out to espionage was severe, the Belgians always kept up this form of patriotic work. It was extremely harmful to us, and its effect could be diminished only by maintaining thorough surveillance of the country in rear of our lines. Our reserves, about which the enemy was always well informed, had for the above reasons to be kept close up behind the front lines in order to be near at hand at the critical moment. Their movements, as well as the sending up of all the necessary

---

[1] *The enemy is giving the Allies credit for his own tricks.*

supplies, were often matters of extreme difficulty. Generally the reserves had to bivouac on sodden meadows, the farms in the neighbourhood being insufficient to provide shelter for them all. The troops who were withdrawn from the front line and put in reserve had therefore small opportunity for either rest or recreation.

The insecurity of our communications back into the interior of Belgium must be passed over almost without mention, except to say that here too a colossal task had been set ; for the weak force allotted to the General-Governor had not only to garrison Belgium, but to provide observation posts along the Dutch frontier. In carrying out these duties, the old *Landsturm* troops showed a spirit of endurance which said much for the military training they had received many years before. The work of keeping watch over the excited population was not without its dangers, and all praise is due to these garrison troops and to the auxiliary troops sent from Germany to their assistance. Thanks to them, the long lines of communication through conquered Belgium were not disturbed, and the supply of the northern wing of our army suffered no interruption from the enemy. For the honour of all concerned this must be put on record.

On the 4th and 7th November the enemy made attacks on a larger scale along the coast. On the 4th, believing that we had left only weak outposts behind, even opposite NIEUPORT, when we retired to the eastern bank of the canal, two to three Belgian regiments advanced through LOMBARTZYDE. At first they gained a slight success, but were shortly afterwards attacked by part of the 38th *Landwehr* Brigade from the east, and by the 33rd *Ersatz* Brigade from the south, and driven back. Detachments of the Marine Division pursued the fleeing Belgians. The second attack made by about five thousand French troops, which took place on the 7th, fared far worse ; the whole of LOMBARTZYDE was taken by our counter-attack, and the enemy losses were very heavy.[1]

On the 9th November the 38th *Landwehr* Brigade was relieved by parts of the Marine Division, for the 10th November was the day on which the new offensive was to be made with fresh troops against YPRES from the south-east.

---

[1] *However, when British troops took over the coastal sector in* 1917 *Lombartzyde was in Allied possession.*

THE LAST PHASE

WHEN the 4th Division and von Winckler's Guard Division were sent forward on the 9th November into the northern part of the fighting line, formerly occupied by the XV Corps, the II Bavarian Corps, from the heights of ST. ELOI it had just stormed, was able to look right down on YPRES. The orders of the Sixth Army commander, dated the 7th and 8th November, had given all the necessary instructions for the employment of the new units. The 4th Infantry Division and von Winckler's Guard Division were placed under the commander of the Guard Corps, General Baron von Plettenberg, and were to be called Plettenberg's Corps. The XV Corps and Plettenberg's Corps formed the Army Group Linsingen.*

The task set the troops of General von Linsingen was 'to drive back and crush the enemy lying north of the canal (COMINES–YPRES); the main weight of the attack is to be delivered by the left wing. The Army Group Fabeck is to maintain its positions west of the canal, its task being to continue pressing forward and at the same time to support the attack of the left wing of the Army Group Linsingen, by as powerful enfilade fire as possible from its right flank batteries.' The decisive attack was to begin on the 10th November, when another strong reinforcement of engineers would

---

* For Order of Battle, see Appendix.

have arrived. All the other units of the Sixth Army and the whole of the Fourth Army were also, according to arrangement, to attack on this day with increased energy, so that the enemy should be allowed no rest, and held to his positions along the whole front.

On the stroke of 7 A.M. the Fourth Army advanced to the attack. This tenth day of November was to be a famous one in its history. The sectors of attack for each of the Corps remained, generally speaking, the same, except that the left wing of the XXVII Reserve Corps had been closed in slightly to the north. Strengthened by the Guard *Jäger* Battalion, a Guard Machine-Gun Detachment [1] and the 9th Machine-Gun Detachment, this Corps was to advance towards the POLYGON Wood.

The orders for the XXII Reserve Corps ran as follows : ' The XXII Reserve Corps * in co-operation with the Marine Division will secure the YSER canal front, and will take DIXMUDE.' Immediately north of DIXMUDE the 4th *Ersatz* Division was in position, with the 43rd Reserve Division to the east and south, the two divisions together making a semicircle of steel round the objective. This time our troops were determined to take the town so stubbornly defended by the French infantry. The enemy fully realised the importance of this bridge-head. Besides holding a strong German force always in the vicinity, it covered the canal-crossing nearest to Calais. On

---

* Consisting of the 4th *Ersatz* Division and the 43rd Reserve Division.

---

[1] *A Machine-Gun Detachment (Abtheilung) is a mounted battery with six guns.*

the 9th its garrison was further reinforced by the arrival of fresh French troops.

The rain of the previous days had made the ground over which the attack on DIXMUDE was to be carried out very heavy going. The HANDZAEME canal, running east and west, divides it into two parts, the northerly one being particularly swampy and difficult to cross. The main attack had therefore to be made from the east and south-east on a comparatively narrow front. The town itself comprised both modern and obsolete fortifications, but the first strongholds of the defenders were the railway buildings and cemetery situated to the east of it. The railway embankment had been transformed into a very strong defensive position, and a heavy fire was expected from it when we advanced from the high embankments of the YSER. Under the cover of darkness the division was able to push its front line to an assault position within two hundred yards of the enemy, and at dawn on the 10th the artillery bombardment began. Our heaviest guns took part and countless shells from our *Minenwerfer* did their utmost to break down the enemy's resistance. By 7.40 A.M. our first attempt to take the enemy's advanced positions had failed, and another artillery bombardment against his obstacles and flanking posts was ordered. At 9.30 A.M. the advanced stronghold at the cemetery was stormed. Our infantry had scarcely got into position there before the artillery observers arrived to direct the fire of their batteries from the front line on to the next strong point. The artillery bombardment lasted throughout the morning until 1 P.M. when the general assault was ordered. The infantry, with detachments of sappers carrying hand-grenades and various material useful in an assault, had worked its way forward close up to the line of obstacles.

The 201st Reserve Infantry Regiment advanced rapidly at first by frontal attack. North of it, the 15th Reserve *Jäger* Battalion under Captain Hameln worked forward across the deep marshes between the canal and the railway. The 202nd Reserve Infantry Regiment came under a heavy enfilade fire from the YSER embankment, and at 1.30 P.M. orders were issued for the Corps reserve under Colonel Teetzmann, consisting of a few battalions of the 43rd Reserve Division and of the 4th *Ersatz* Division, to be brought up into the line. Its task was to help carry forward the attack of the 202nd Regiment against the railway embankment, and to secure the left flank of the advance. The nearer the attack approached to the town, the more desperate became the resistance of its defenders. The gallant commander of the 201st Reserve Regiment, General von Seydewitz, always in the front line encouraging his men, was killed leading the attack just as his regiment and the *Jäger* entered the devastated town at about 3.30 P.M. Our well-directed artillery fire had cleared the front at the critical moment, and the enemy withdrew to the flanks of and behind DIXMUDE, but did not cease to offer resistance. He held the railway embankment south of the town with particular tenacity. Even when this had been finally stormed, the 202nd Regiment had to continue the fight, with heavy loss, among the burning houses in the southern part of the town, until the 201st Regiment by a wheel southwards were able to give assist-

ance. Teetzmann's brigade in its attack on the
YSER embankment, to protect the flank of the division, had meanwhile reached the river. Thence it
pressed on towards the bridges west of the town, so
that the enemy's retreat was threatened. In spite
of this, however, he gave nothing up without a
struggle, and every block of houses had to be captured : in fact the street fighting that ensued was
hardly less bitter and terrible than at WYTSCHAETE
and MESSINES.

During the struggle in DIXMUDE, the French
artillery fired into the place regardless of friend or
foe, and both suffered alike. The fight was still
raging among the houses at the northern exit, where
von Beerst was only making slow progress with the
advanced detachments of the 4th *Ersatz* Division,
when our reserves were assembled in the market-
square to deliver the final blow. The French infantry
and Marine Fusiliers put up a desperate defence, but
finally had to give way, for though not numerically
superior, the offensive spirit of the German troops
overcame all resistance. It was not until the west
bank of the canal had been reached, that the mass
of the enemy put up another defence.

DIXMUDE was captured, and the French had been
driven back across the canal. A combined counter-
attack by Belgians, Zouaves and French, which began
during the evening and continued into the night,
was unable to alter the situation, and though DIX-
MUDE in consequence was under the heaviest fire,
our troops held their ground. Weak detachments
of the 4th *Ersatz* Division were even able to cross
the river north of the town under cover of darkness,

though the extreme swampiness of the ground prevented them carrying their success any further. The
enemy had prepared the bridges, west of DIXMUDE,
for demolition some time before and had constructed
strong positions along the west bank of the YSER.

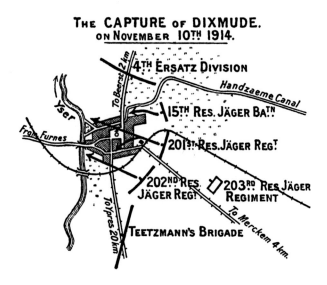

These were especially good, as the ground there is
higher and overlooks that on the east bank. Our
artillery had therefore to make another preparatory
bombardment. The spoils taken at DIXMUDE were
considerable, and in spite of the fact that the British
assert that the Allies only lost a few hundred men,
we took in prisoners alone 17 officers and 1400 men.[1]

---

[1] *It is not clear why a British assertion about the defence of Dixmude
should be quoted, nor indeed is it clear what shape this assertion can have
taken, as no British troops were concerned in the Dixmude fighting, nor
could there have been any occasion for any official British announce-
ment about Dixmude.*

*In the diagram above, for 201st, 202nd, and 203rd Res. Jäger Regt.
read Res. Infantry Regt.*

Our allied enemies had also been driven back over the canal, south of DIXMUDE, on the 10th November. The XXIII Reserve Corps had made a successful attack on NOORDSCHOOTE and through BIXSCHOOTE against HET SAS. A long and bitter struggle took place for the high ground south-west of BIXSCHOOTE ; but by evening the canal had been reached along almost its whole length between NOORDSCHOOTE and BIXSCHOOTE, whilst about a brigade of the 45th Reserve Division and weak detachments of the 46th had crossed it. The inundation had however gradually extended southwards as far as this district, and put any far-reaching extension of this success out of the question. The XXIII Reserve Corps took prisoner about 1000 men and captured a considerable number of machine-guns in this operation.

The reinforced III Reserve Corps had had a particularly hard fight on both sides of LANGEMARCK. Throughout the 9th November and during the following night the French delivered heavy attacks there and had been everywhere repulsed. Rows of corpses lay in front of the III Reserve Corps, on the left wing of which the 9th Reserve Division, now affiliated to the Fourth Army, had been brought up into the line. Making every use of the element of surprise, General von Beseler had ordered the assault to begin at 6.30 A.M. Punctually at this moment, as dawn was breaking, the bugles sounded the attack. On the right wing the 44th Reserve Division pushed forward till close up to HET SAS, taking prisoner 14 officers and 1154 men. The official despatch, in reporting this advance, says : 'West of LANGE-MARCK our young regiments advanced against the enemy's front line singing "*Deutschland, Deutschland über alles*," and captured it.' The left wing of the division hung a good way back, as the 5th Reserve Division on its left was unable to push on so rapidly. It had broken into the enemy's first position, but its eastern wing was completely held up in front of LANGEMARCK. The 6th Reserve Division had attacked the place from north and east, without being able to take it. Documents discovered afterwards prove that the enemy had concentrated strong forces here for a big attack that he himself intended to make on the 10th, and these were now defending every yard of ground with the utmost determination. The 9th Reserve Division had at first made good progress in the direction of ST. JULIEN, but it came under a heavy cross-fire, and was thereby compelled to give up a large part of the ground gained. General von Beseler therefore decided to pull out the main body of the 9th Reserve Division, and move it to his right wing, where the 44th and 5th Reserve Divisions had had a decided success in the direction of HET SAS.

After the first line of trenches had been taken, the attack of the XXVI and XXVII Reserve Corps was very soon held up by wire entanglements which had not been destroyed by our guns, and by a second line of trenches provided with every modern device. The XXVII Reserve Corps spent most of the day in making such disposition of its forces as would enable it to give the utmost support to the Army Group Linsingen, which was getting ready to attack further south on the morrow.

In the Army Group Linsingen, however, the preparations of Plettenberg's Corps for an offensive on

the morning of the 10th were not sufficiently advanced
to allow it to take place on that day.   Further, the
dense autumn mists prevented the necessary recon-
naissances.   With the concurrence of General von
Linsingen, and after arrangement with the neighbouring troops, General Baron von Plettenberg therefore decided to attack on the 11th November.   On
the front of Deimling's (XV) Corps the 10th November,
up to four in the afternoon, was spent in a preparatory
artillery bombardment ;   especially good work was
done by means of heavy enfilade fire from the south,
carried out by a massed group of artillery consisting
of three batteries of heavy howitzers, three batteries
of mortars, a battery of 10-cm. guns and a battery
of long 15-cm. guns, all under the orders of Colonel
Gartmayr, commanding the 1st Bavarian Field
Artillery Regiment.   After the bombardment both
divisions of the Corps advanced to the attack and,
in co-operation with the II Bavarian Corps fighting
on the high ground of St. Eloi, were able to gain
some hundreds of yards.

On the 11th November the combined offensive of
the Fourth Army and the Army Groups Linsingen
and Fabeck took place.   The remainder of the Fourth
and Sixth Armies continued their attacks.   The
great efforts made by the Fourth Army on the 10th
had considerably weakened it, and further handi-
capped by a heavy rain-storm which beat in the faces
of the attacking troops, no special success was gained
by it on the 11th ;   nevertheless the enemy was everywhere held to his ground and prevented from trans-
ferring any troops to other parts of the front.   On the
extreme right wing the Marine Division made a suc-

cessful attack on NIEUPORT, capturing several hundred
prisoners.   At the same time the Guard Cavalry Division, affiliated to the Fourth Army, was sent up to

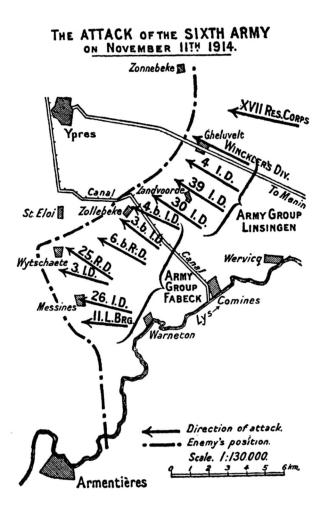

THE ATTACK OF THE SIXTH ARMY
ON NOVEMBER 11TH 1914.

the YSER, in order to relieve part of the 4th *Ersatz*
Division, which went into Army Reserve.   On the
left wing of the Army, the XXVI and XXVII Reserve

Corps worked their way towards the hostile positions by sapping, whilst the units on the extreme south flank of the XXVII Reserve Corps attacked in close co-operation with Plettenberg's Corps.

On the 11th, in pouring rain, the Army Groups Linsingen and Fabeck began the last phase of this severe and terrible struggle for YPRES ; and it was destined to fix the general line on which the opposing armies were to remain rooted till the spring of 1915.

Von Winckler's Guard Division fought on the right wing of the Army Group Linsingen, and for us the day was to be a historic, though costly one. In former wars the Guard had always been in the heat of the fray at its most critical stages, and the sons were to show themselves worthy of their fathers. The spirit of Frederick the Great and the glory of St. Privat shone again on the battlefield of YPRES. The British speak of the attack of the Guard as a most brilliant feat of arms.

Before the infantry of the Division could come into immediate contact with the enemy, a broad zone had to be crossed under his artillery fire : through the hail of shell the pride and iron discipline of the Guard brought its regiments unshaken. At 7.30 A.M. the German batteries opened, and a furious bombardment continued for two and a half hours, and then the infantry attack began. It struck against two divisions of the I British Corps, a war experienced foe, whose fighting methods were well adapted to the country.[1] The artillery preparation however had

---

[1] *The frontage attacked by the twelve battalions of General von Winckler's Guard Division, far from being held by two British Divisions was held from north to south by the 1st Infantry Brigade, now reduced*

been a thorough one, and in spite of the enemy's superiority in numbers the advance made good progress, so that shortly after 10 A.M. the strong position along the southern edge of the POLYGON Wood was in the possession of the 3rd Guard Regiment.[1]

At the same time the butt ends and bayonets of H.M. the Emperor's 1st Guard Regiment had forced a way through the wire entanglements and trenches in front of VERBECK farm, and it was taken in the first assault. The regiment had thereby captured an excellent position from which to support the right wing of the attack.[2] Led by its fearless commander, Prince Eitel Friedrich of Prussia, it then pressed on without a moment's delay into the wood north-west of the farm. Meanwhile the 3rd Guard Regiment was still engaged along the southern edges of the woods

---

to some 800 *bayonets, a battalion of Zouaves and the left brigade of the 3rd Division, little over* 1200 *strong. Even if the whole of the 3rd Guard Regiment may have been absorbed in the task of covering the main attack from the British troops lining the southern edge of the Polygon Wood, the superiority of the attacking force was sufficiently pronounced.*

[1] *The Germans do not appear to have penetrated into the Polygon Wood at any point. The northern end of the breach in the British line was marked by a ' strong point ' which had been erected near the south-west corner of the wood, known later as ' Black Watch Corner ' : this was successfully defended all day by a very weak company of the Black Watch. Attacks were made on the 1st King's lining the southern edge of the wood, apparently by the 3rd Guard Regiment, and also further eastward and to the left of the King's, on the 2nd Coldstream Guards. The Germans in this quarter would seem to have belonged to the 54th Reserve Division : at neither of these points did the attackers meet with any success.*

[2] *A thick mist which prevented the troops holding the front line trenches from seeing far to their front undoubtedly played an important part in concealing the advance of the German Guard, and contributed appreciably to its success.*

west of REUTEL, with its front facing north, and it
put in its last reserves to help forward the left wing
of the 54th Reserve Division.

At 10 A.M., on the last artillery salvo, the battalions
of the 4th Guard Brigade advanced to the assault on

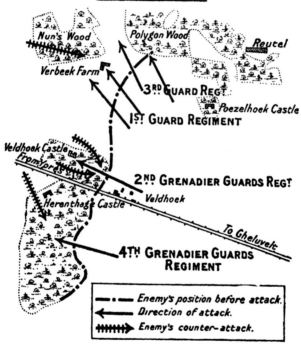

THE ATTACK OF THE 2ND GUARD DIVISION.
ON NOVEMBER 11TH 1914.

both sides of the YPRES–GHELUVELT main road,
and they took the front British trenches in their
stride.

The Emperor Francis' 2nd Guard Grenadier Regiment attacked from VELDHOEK against the corner

of the HERENTHAGE Wood, north of the YPRES–
GHELUVELT road, and took its edge. The wood itself
gave the infantry endless trouble, for it was impossible
to see a yard ahead in its thick undergrowth, which
was over six feet high.[1] Suddenly at a few paces'
distance, machine-guns would open on our troops
from behind a bush or a tree-trunk. Thus the task
set the Grenadiers proved to be an extremely difficult
one, the more so as they had lost many of their officers
and N.C.O.'s in the first rush across the open. Nevertheless, the defence-works inside the wood were quickly
taken one after another, but more strong points protected by wire entanglements untouched by our
artillery fire were encountered. The Fusilier Battalion
forced its way through to the château of VELDHOEK,
which was surrounded by a marsh and an impenetrable hedge. The men were trying to work their
way one by one through the latter by cutting gaps in
it, when suddenly a deafening roar of rifle and machine-
gun burst upon them. It came from the château on
their right, from some flanking trenches on their left,
and from trees behind the line. A number of the
few remaining officers fell, and finally the battalion
had to retire a short distance in order to reorganise.
But it soon came forward once more, and the companies pressed on till they were close up to the château
itself, when another annihilating fusillade was opened
on them from all sides. Simultaneously the British
made a flank attack along the hedge in order to cut
off the men who had got through. Machine-guns

---

[1] *This is the eastern part of the wood known later as ' Inverness
Copse.'*

firing from trees and from the château windows completely stopped any communication with them. Very few only of these foremost troops, who were commanded by Captain von Rieben, succeeded in getting away. Those who did were assembled by Captain Baron von Sell at the eastern edge of the wood and were, with part of the 1st Battalion, led forward again to the relief of the Fusiliers who were surrounded. The attack of Captain von Sell developed however into small isolated combats, and though the boldest followed their leader nearly up to the château again, they were received there with such heavy fire from right and left that it appeared that they would have to retire again and reorganise. Before this could be carried out, a British counter-attack was launched; but our men, disorganised and mixed up as they were, held fast to their ground and stopped the attack, although at first both their flanks were in the air.[1]

Queen Augusta's 4th Guard Grenadier Regiment, advancing south of the main road, at once suffered such heavy losses that the first two attacks made no headway. When however part of the regiment near the main road pushed forward along it, echeloned behind its sister-regiment on the right, and then turned southwards, the advance made good progress, and a firm footing was gained in HERENTHAGE Wood south of the road. The reverses met with by the Emperor Francis' 2nd Grenadiers unfortunately enabled the British to bring such a heavy enfilade fire to bear

---

[1] *This counter-attack may be identified with one delivered by the 1st Scots Fusiliers and one company 2nd Duke of Wellington's.*

on Queen Augusta's 4th Grenadiers, that their advance had to be stopped.[1]

At 5 P.M. German Guard troops had a tussle with the British Guards. The King's Liverpool Regiment made a counter-attack from the NUN's Wood (Nonne Bosch) against the extreme left of the 1st Guard Foot Regiment and the northern wing of the 2nd Guard Grenadiers. The point of attack was well chosen, and took both the regiments in flank, for the 1st Guard Infantry Brigade was at this time heavily engaged, and held up in the woods (POLYGON Wood and the eastern part of the NONNE BOSCH), with its front facing north, and the 2nd Guard Grenadier Regiment, having spent all its energies against the château of VELDHOEK, lay with its front facing west.[2] However, the British

---

[1] *The 4th (Queen Augusta's) Guard Grenadiers seem to have attacked the right of the line held by the 9th Infantry Brigade and to have been repulsed by the 1st Lincolnshires and 1st Northumberland Fusiliers. Further to the British right the 15th and 7th Infantry Brigades were also attacked, but by the 4th Division, not by the Guards. Here the Germans made no progress.*

[2] *This part of the German account is not borne out by the British versions. The main body of the 1st Guard Regiment, which broke through the thinly held line of the 1st Infantry Brigade, pressed on north-west into the Nonne Bosch Wood, pushing right through it, and coming out into the open on the western edge. Here their progress was arrested mainly by the gunners of XLI Brigade, R.F.A., who held them up with rifle fire at short range. Various details of Royal Engineers, orderlies from Headquarters, transport men, rallied stragglers of the 1st Brigade, assisted to stop the Germans, but the situation was critical until about noon or a little later the 2nd Oxford and Bucks L.I. arrived on the scene. This battalion had been engaged for several days near Zwarteleen, and had just been brought up to Westhoek to act as Divisional Reserve. Though under 400 strong the battalion promptly counter-attacked the Nonne Bosch Wood and drove the Germans out headlong. Many of them were caught as they escaped on the eastern and southern sides by the fire of the 2nd Highland L.I., now on the western edge of Polygon*

troops ran into their own artillery fire near the NONNE
BOSCH, and the attack broke up and came to a standstill in front of our thin and scattered lines. Any
further advance on the 11th November by our Guard
troops north of the road was now out of the question.

In the southern part of the HERENTHAGE Wood the
4th Infantry Division pushed on, though here too
great difficulties were encountered. Deep trenches,
broad obstacles, and enfilade machine-gun fire combined to make our progress slow, especially on the
right wing.

The XV Corps in close co-operation with the left
wing of the Pomeranians gained ground in the woods
near and around ZWARTELEEN ; the capture of Hill
60 near ZWARTELEEN was of exceptional importance.
From this elevation another direct view over the
country round YPRES was obtained.

South of the canal the II Bavarian Corps with much
thinned ranks stormed forward again. The bit of

---

*Wood, and of the 1st Northamptonshires, who had come up to Glencorse
Wood, south-west of the Nonne Bosch, and with other units of the
2nd and 3rd Infantry Brigades had filled the gap which extended thence
to the Menin road. Thus those of the 1st Guard Regiment who had
pushed straight on westward were prevented from penetrating any
further. The King's, to whom this account gives the credit for the
Oxfordshire's counter-attack, had been engaged with the 3rd Guard
Regiment further to the north, completely defeating their attacks on the
Polygon, but not making any counter-attack. It is worth recalling that
at the critical moment of the battle of Waterloo it was the 2nd Oxford
and Bucks L.I., then 52nd Light Infantry, who played the chief part
in the defeat of Napoleon's Guard.*

*The defeat of the 2nd Guard Grenadiers does not appear to have
been the work of the 2nd Oxford and Bucks L.I., but of the other battalions, chiefly from the 2nd and 3rd Infantry Brigades, who were
pushed forward rather earlier between Glencorse Wood and Inverness
Copse.*

wood north-east of WYTSCHAETE, which had already
changed hands several times, was now taken by it.
The heavy artillery again rendered invaluable services.
Several strong hostile counter-attacks were held up
chiefly owing to the way in which at the critical
moment our guns always protected the infantry lines
by a barrage.

In the area near WYTSCHAETE, the 11th November
was the day of the heaviest fighting. In the woods
north of it, Bavarians and Hessians pressed forward
together, slowly but surely. A French battery and
four machine-guns were taken by the 168th Infantry
Regiment at a farm about 150 yards north of WYT-
SCHAETE, but the guns were so firmly embedded in
the sodden ground, that they could not be got away
by the infantry. When the buildings were evacuated
again, owing to the heavy fire of the French on them,
the guns, made unserviceable by us, remained as a
neutral battery between the lines. It must be re-
corded here that in the fight for one single farm the
Hessians took prisoners belonging to three different
regiments, a fact that proves what masses the enemy
had put in to the fight on the YPRES front, and to
what an extent he had to concentrate his units to
ward off our attacks.

On and to the west of the MESSINES ridge the line
remained almost unaltered during the 11th November.
The very severe effect of the enemy's artillery fire
from Mount KEMMEL on this front and the enfilade
fire of artillery and machine-guns from PLOEGSTEERT
Wood compelled our men to remain in their trenches.

Taken as a whole the operations on the 11th November were a great success. A series of brilliant feats,

many of which it has been impossible even to mention in this short account, far less adequately describe, gave us unchallenged possession of positions from which any concentration of the enemy near YPRES could be seen, and immediately opened on by artillery. It is true, however, that no break through of the enemy's lines had been accomplished : his numerical superiority and, more especially, the strength of his positions held up our offensive. The weather conditions, storm and rain, had also contributed towards the result.[1]

The furious character of the fighting on the 11th November did not abate on the following day, but on the whole the situation remained unaltered. The general character of the operations on the entire front of the Fourth and Sixth Armies was now changed, and sapping was eventually resorted to, though here and there successes in open warfare were gained. For instance the XXII Reserve Corps managed to strengthen its detachments across the YSER at DIX-MUDE, and on the 12th the 201st Reserve Infantry

---

[1] *The author must be thankful for minor mercies if he can reckon 11th November as a day of great success. The gain of ground at Veld-hoek was trifling in extent and value, and though ' Hill 60 ' and the wood north of Wytschaete were more important points, there is no doubt that the throwing of the German Guard into the struggle had been expected to produce a break-through. The ' numerical superiority ' once again attributed to the Allies was about as unreal as the alleged strength of the positions, hastily dug, imperfectly wired and almost wholly lacking supporting points and communications, which had such a much more formidable character in the eyes of the Germans than they ever possessed in reality. The gallantry and vigour with which the German Guard pushed its attack will be readily admitted, but the honours of 11th November 1914 go to the weary men who after three weeks of incessant fighting met and drove back these fresh and famous troops.*

Regiment, under Major Baron von Wedekind, stormed the enemy's defences opposite it on the western bank of the YSER, and held them under great difficulties. Constant rain had filled the badly constructed trenches with mud so that our troops had to support the enemy's bombardment and resist his counter-attacks lying in the open.

At BIXSCHOOTE the enemy again attempted strong counter-attacks, but they were stopped largely by the muddy state of the country. On the 14th November there was a recrudescence of severe fighting. Owing to the misty weather our relieving troops occupied a reserve position instead of the original front line ; by the time the error was discovered, our watchful opponents were already in the front German position. Our men, however, gave them no rest there, for their honour would not suffer the surrender in this manner of their success of the 10th November. Without waiting for any orders from higher authority or for reinforcements they attacked and retook the strong position on the rising ground south-west of BIXSCHOOTE. On the front of the Sixth Army HEREN-THAGE Wood was completely taken by the Guard on the 14th November after severe hand-to-hand fighting.[1]

---

[1] *This statement is not true. After an attack on 13th November in which prisoners were taken from the 4th (German) Division, the 9th and 15th Infantry Brigades drew back from the eastern edge of the Herenthage Wood to a line about 200 yards in rear (night 13th-14th November). This line was strongly attacked next day, and the Herenthage Château fell for the time into German hands, only to be recovered by the 2nd King's Own Yorkshire L.I., while a further counter-attack by a company of the Northumberland Fusiliers, assisted by a gun of the 54th Battery R.F.A., ousted the Germans also from the stables of the Château. Further to the British right the 7th and 15th Infantry Brigades successfully repulsed vigorous attacks.*

After the artillery had prepared the way as far as was possible in that difficult and wooded neighbourhood, the infantry, whose fighting spirit was by no means damped by the events of the 11th November, advanced to the assault. In the château of HEREN-THAGE a large number of British snipers surrendered. The XV Corps had another success in the wooded district of ZWARTELEEN after being reinforced by Hofmann's composite Division. A strong system of trenches and dug-outs were taken, as well as a large number of prisoners.

On the 13th November the Park of WYTSCHAETE was captured from the French by the Pomeranians and Bavarians. A counter-attack, in which the French advanced against our positions shouting, 'Don't shoot,' in German, cost them heavy losses ; and the Bavarians, whose tempers were roused by this treachery, drove them back to their original positions.

On the 20th November the farm 150 yards north of WYTSCHAETE, for which such a severe fight had been made on the 11th, was finally captured by us. We thereby obtained a position in the WYTSCHAETE salient which, although overlooked from Mount KEMMEL, gave us such a commanding view of all the ground between Mount KEMMEL and the WYT-SCHAETE–MESSINES ridge that surprise attacks by the enemy in this district were now out of the question.[1] On the rest of the Flanders front only small fights took place, and on the 17th November the commander of the Fourth Army decided to give up any

---

[1] *The surprise came in 1917 in spite of this.*

idea of continuing the offensive ; a decision to which he was compelled by the low fighting strength of his troops and the bad autumn weather, which was affecting their health.[1] The frequent downpours of rain during November had caused a constant rising of the water-level, and it became urgently necessary to provide regular reliefs for the troops, for they were worn out by the constant fighting under such bad weather conditions. Clear signs of exhaustion in the enemy's ranks on the front opposite the Fourth and Sixth Armies were also noticed. This permitted our gallant Fourth Army gradually to construct a good line of trenches and erect wire entanglements. As soon as these were completed rest-billets were allotted further to the rear and the men found quiet and pleasant quarters in the villages of Flanders untouched by war, with a not unfriendly population. The German General Staff fully concurred in the decision of the commander of the Fourth Army made on the 17th November. They at the same time expressed the hope that the Army would be prepared to hold its positions even against superior hostile forces. This expectation was completely fulfilled by the Fourth Army, and although at that time there were four and one-half French Corps, as well as the 25,000 Belgian troops, opposed to the forces of Duke Albert of Wür-

---

[1] *One reason why the G.O.C. Fourth Army came to this decision on 17th November is omitted. An attack in force had been attempted on this day by his 4th Division, but the 7th and 15th Infantry Brigades, holding the line attacked, had proved equal to the occasion, had driven the Germans back, recovering some advanced trenches carried by the first rush and inflicting heavy losses. This discouraging reception undoubtedly assisted Duke Albert in making his decision.*

temburg, they never obtained a success of any consequence.

The threat against our right flank ceased soon afterwards. British monitors appeared a few times towards the end of November off the roadstead of OSTEND. They bombarded the canal exit and our positions near by : but their fire was as ineffective as before. The 'glorious' activities of the British Grand Fleet along the Flanders coast came to a speedy end as soon as our ill-famed sea-rats, the U-boats, began to put in an appearance there.[1]

The developments on the front of the Sixth Army during the second half of November 1914 were similar to those of the Fourth Army. For some time the sapping was continued, but from the 20th onwards strong detachments were taken from it and entrained for the Eastern Front, where General von Hindenburg was able, in the fighting round Lodz, to bring the Russian steam-roller to a standstill, and finally make it roll back again.

From this time onwards the line of demarcation between the Fourth and Sixth Armies was the COMINES–YPRES canal.

---

[1] *It was the U-boats that came to a speedy end.*

CONCLUSION

As the November storms passed and frost and icy winds heralded to the mild climate of Flanders the approach of winter, the unbroken defensive lines of both sides were being slowly strengthened. The effect of artillery fire compelled them to make cover in good trenches and behind thick breast - works. As the armament in use became more and more power-ful, artificial shelter, where the surface water allowed it, had to be made deeper and deeper in the earth. At first passive defence was little understood by the German troops, as instruction in the offensive had dominated all other in their peace-training, and in the short period available after they were called up the volunteers had only been trained in the prin-ciples of attack. Their sense of superiority over their opponents did not let them rest content with merely holding positions. The high sense of duty in each individual was of assistance, and the methods of defensive warfare were quickly learnt. The con-tinuous bad weather in the autumn and winter in this water-logged country caused great suffering; and the troops sent off to Russia to fight under the great victor of TANNENBURG were much envied. The despatch of men eastward showed those left behind that any hope of a final decision at YPRES had dis-appeared.

The first battle of YPRES was a German victory,[1] for it marked the failure of the enemy's intention to fall on the rear of our Western Armies, to free the rich districts of Northern France and the whole of Belgium (thus preventing us from making use of their valuable resources), and to use the YPRES area as a base for the Belgian, French and British advance on the RHINE. The Belgian coast was now firmly in our possession, and offered a good starting-place for naval operations against England. But we had not succeeded in making the decisive break-through, and the dream of ending the campaign in the west in our favour during 1914 had to be consigned to its grave. It is only natural that the German General Staff found it difficult thoroughly to realise this unpleasant fact, and only did so with reluctance ; but endeavour has been made in this account to bring out the main reasons which led to this result of the battle. Nevertheless, great things had been accomplished. The Army of Duke Albert of Würtemburg, by its advance and determined attack, had prevented the big offensive planned by the enemy ; the Fourth and Sixth Armies together had forced a superior opponent into the defensive, and, in spite of his having called in the sea to his assistance, had driven him back continually, until positions had been reached which enabled German troops to be spared to carry out an offensive on the Eastern Front. As during the battle of the Marne, so now the spectre of a Russian invasion appeared threateningly before the German Nation, and the whole country knew what it would mean if it should materialise. Our forces on the Eastern

---

[1] *See remarks in Introduction.*

Front were far too weak, and even the genius of a Hindenburg could not decisively defeat the masses of the Grand Duke Nicolas without reinforcements. Thus it came about that we had to lie and wait in front of the gates of YPRES, while all the available men from Flanders were hurried across to Poland, to help Hindenburg pave the way to victory.

There was never peace on the YPRES front. The belt of steel with which we had invested the town by our operations in October and November 1914, was a source of constant annoyance to the British, whilst our position on the Belgian coast seemed to our cousins across the Channel like an apparition whose shadow lay over the British Isles and especially menaced the traffic-routes between England and France. The British therefore continually tried their utmost to free themselves of this menace and their pressure produced counter measures. Thus in December 1914 heavy fighting again occurred, especially near the sea at NIEUPORT, and also at BIXSCHOOTE and ZWAR-TELEEN. On Christmas Eve the French vainly attacked BIXSCHOOTE : their hope of catching the Germans dreaming heavily on that evening was of no avail. When spring lifted the mist that hung over Flanders, a German offensive took place during April and May that forced the northern part of the YPRES salient back to within three miles of the town.[1] After this the positions only altered very slightly. In March 1916 the British blew up our front trench positions at ST. ELOI by five colossal mines, but were

---

[1] *The first use of gas by the Germans on this occasion might have been mentioned.*

unable to hold on to the ground thus destroyed. In 1917 the death-agony of YPRES was renewed, and for months war raged over the plains of Flanders ; the fighting was as furious as in October and November 1914. The young soldiers of those days have now become veterans, who know war and do not fear it even in its most terrible forms. The enemy are those same British against whom Crown Prince Rupert of Bavaria, in exhorting the troops to battle in 1914, once said : ' Therefore when you are fighting this particular enemy retaliate for his deceit and for having occasioned all this great sacrifice ; show him that the Germans are not so easy to wipe out of the world's history as he imagines, show it by redoubling the strength behind your blows. In front of you is the opponent who is the greatest obstacle to peace. On ! at him ! '

He spoke as a prophet. Hate of the British who were so jealous of us, who brought on the war for the sake of their money-bags and spread the conflagration all over the world, who at first hoped that it would be but necessary to pour out their silver bullets to annihilate Germany : all this steeled the hearts of our warriors in Flanders, whose creed was the justice of the German cause. And the British efforts to wrest Flanders away from us again were stifled in mud and in blood. The fighting in 1917 was perhaps more severe than that of those stormy autumn days of 1914, but the objective for us was ever the same : to keep the enemy far, far from our homes. In this we succeeded in 1917 as in 1914.

Flanders ! The word is heard by every one in the German Fatherland with a silent shudder, but also with just and intense pride. It was there that the British were made to realise that German heroism was not to be vanquished, not even by the use of the war material which the whole world had been manufacturing for years. When we read that up to the 14th November 1914, 40 divisions had been put into the battle round YPRES by the Western Allies, whilst only 25 German divisions were opposed to them,[1] and that in the course of the Flanders battle of 1917, 99 British and French divisions struggled in vain against a greatly inferior German force, it says much for our troops. But far from all. For the enemy's superiority in material, in guns, trench-mortars, machine-guns, aeroplanes, etc., was two, three, and even fourfold. Who can doubt but that a nation whose sons know how to fight like this, must win ? Let us only hold the hope that the seeds of blood sown in Flanders will bring forth rich and splendid fruit for the German Fatherland. This indeed would be the highest reward that could be bestowed on those of us who fought there.

---

[1] *It is not to be read in this monograph. See Introduction.*

APPENDIX

ORDER OF BATTLE OF THE FOURTH ARMY
from 10th Oct. 1914 to 16th Nov. 1914.

Commander . . General Duke Albert of Würtemburg.

Chief of Staff . . Major-General Ilse.

III Reserve Corps . (General of Infantry von Beseler).
5th Reserve Division.
6th Reserve Division.
4th *Ersatz* Division.

XXII Reserve Corps . (General of Cavalry von Falkenhayn).
43rd Reserve Division.
44th Reserve Division.

XXIII Reserve Corps . (General of Cavalry von Kleist).
45th Reserve Division.
46th Reserve Division.

XXVI Reserve Corps . (General of Infantry von Hügel).
51st Reserve Division.
52nd Reserve Division.

XXVII Reserve Corps . (Lieut.-General von Carlowitz, relieved on 27th Oct. by General of Artillery von Schubert).
53rd (Saxon) Reserve Division.
54th (Würtemburg) Reserve Division.

The following units were also attached at various times :—
9th Reserve Division.
6th Bavarian Reserve Division.
Marine Division.
38th *Landwehr* Brigade.
37th *Landwehr* Brigade.
2nd *Ersatz* Brigade.
Guard Cavalry Division.

ORDER OF BATTLE OF THE ARMY GROUP FABECK
from 27th Oct. 1914 to 20th Nov. 1914.

Commander . . General of Infantry von Fabeck, Commanding XIII (Würtemburg) Corps.

Chief of Staff . . Lieut.-Colonel von Lossberg.

XV Corps . . . (General von Deimling).
30th Infantry Division.
39th Infantry Division.
(This Corps left the Army Group Fabeck on the 8th Nov. 1914.)

II Bavarian Corps . (General of Infantry von Martini, relieved on the 5th Nov. 1914 by General of Cavalry von Stetten).
3rd Bavarian Infantry Division.
4th Bavarian Infantry Division.

26th (Würtemburg) Infantry Division . (Lieut.-General William, Duke of Urach).

Group GEROK was also temporarily in the Army Group FABECK.

ORDER OF BATTLE OF THE GROUP GEROK

Commander . . General of Infantry von Gerok,
Commanding **XXIV** Reserve
Corps.

1st Cavalry Corps . (Lieut.-General von Richthofen).
2 Cavalry Divisions.[1]

2nd Cavalry Corps . (General of Cavalry von der
Marwitz).
2 Cavalry Divisions.[2]

6th Bavarian Reserve Division.

3rd Infantry Division.

25th Reserve Division.

11th *Landwehr* Brigade.

2nd Cavalry Division.

Bavarian Cavalry Division.

ORDER OF BATTLE OF THE ARMY GROUP LINSINGEN

from 8th Nov. 1914 to 18th Nov. 1914.

Commander . . General of Infantry von Linsingen,
Commanding II Corps.

Chief of Staff . . Colonel von Hammerstein-
Gesmold.

---

[1] *4th and Guard Cavalry Divisions* (*see page* 64).

[2] *3rd and 7th Cavalry Divisions* (*see page* 90).

XV Corps . . . (General of Infantry von Deimling).
        30th Infantry Division.
        39th Infantry Division.
also from 16th Nov., Hofmann's Composite Division.

Plettenberg's Corps . (General of Infantry von Plettenberg, Commanding Guard Corps).
        4th Infantry Division.
        Winckler's Composite Guard Division.

INDEX

135